Further Cryptozoolo

being a supplement to A Dictionary of
Cryptozoology *and* Cryptosup

Ronan Coghlan

BANGOR:
XIPHOS BOOKS
2007

Published by:-

Xiphos Books,
1, Hillside Gardens,
Bangor,
Northern Ireland,
BT19 6SJ.

ISBN: 978 09544936-8-4

First Edition.

Introduction

This volume is essentially a supplement to two previous works, *A Dictionary of Cryptozoology* (2004) and *Cryptosup* (2005). In the main, it contains articles on creatures not covered by these two volumes, but it also contains additions and updates to articles within those works.

This work looks on cryptozoology from a folkloric point of view and therefore contains, not alone cryptids which might exist, but also cryptids which have never existed, but have been the objects of belief.

Cryptozoology insofar as this work is concerned encompasses:-

   (a) mystery animals which possibly exist
   (b) paranormal creatures allegedly witnessed
   (c) mythological creatures wholly the product of human imagination
   (d) supposedly extinct creatures that may yet survive or certain creatures whose present existence is somewhat doubtful.

In addition, I have extended my remit somewhat into cryptobotany, the study of mystery plants.

ADIYAMAN CREATURES Small figures seen by farmers in Turkey in 2001. They were described as having large heads and red feet - the figures, not the farmers. [224]

AFRICAN CHUPACABRAS The term applied, probably quite erroneously, to an unseen and unidentified predator in Namibia, which has been killing livestock around Okakarara. Its tracks indicate it can cover five metres at a jump. These tracks look like the heel of a foot. [12]

AGRICAULANDIA CREATURE Strange creature seen by a cyclist in Brazil in 2005. It was dark and hairy with short thick legs and jumped over a fence. [224]

ALABAMA GOATMAN A goatman, about 7' in height, has been reported from the state of Alabama.

ALAOTRA GREBE A bird (*Tachybaptus rufolavatus*) which was last reported with certainty in 1985. It is now thought probably, but not certainly, extinct. [www.birdlife.com]

ALASKAN BIG CAT A mysterious big

cat, about the size of a German shepherd/Alsatian and coloured similarly, reported from a sighting in Alaska at an unspecified date. This is beyond the puma's range and the witness was certain it wasn't a lynx. [2]

ALIEN BIG CAT As in *Cryptosup,* we shall exclude alleged sightings of black and brown cats like panthers and pumas, as sightings of creatures such as these are now so numerous. Merrily Harpur now contends that ABCs seen in Britain are preternatural creatures of the kind called *daimons* by the Greeks. This word is usually rendered *daemon* in English. (It should not be confused with *demon*). With regard to ABCs' possible identity as giant ferals, noted zoologist Maurice Burton one studied a feral cat which he described as enormous. Similarly, a big cat killed in Australia was also shown to be a large feral domestic, thanks to DNA analysis. It measured 6' in length including the tail. ABCs listed in this little work will be those of more unusual colours.

ALMAS *Add to Dictionary article* What was apparently the almas was referred to in a book published as early as 1420 by

German writer Hans Schiltberger, but it did not become well-known in the West until 1958-9. However, the noted writer N. Przewalski claimed to have seen a number of almas in 1871.

ALOM-BAG-WINNO-SIS Water-dwelling creature in the traditions of the Abenaki Indians.

ALVIN MONSTER This creature was seen from the submersible *Alvin.* The witness said it was living and 40'-50' long at least, but he had no desire to initiate further investigation. [B]

AMARU Dragon or snake of Incan legend. [190]

AMAZON DINOSAUR A bipedal reptile which A. Mesquita told naturalist R. Blomberg he had seen. [191]

AMERICAN GIANT The existence of giant humans on the American continent has been inferred from the alleged exhumation of bones, but these do not seem to have survived. However, in 1528 Cabeza de Vaca was alleged to have fought with giants on the American continent. The

Cocope Indians believed in a race of giants with a taste for cannibalism, though not all of them practised it. These giants, they aver, were four times the size of a man, but their women were of about human stature. They say that, within historical times, a giant attacked a man on the Wisconsin River. Some of them say the giants died out about 1840.

AMERICAN LION *Add to Dictionary article* With regard to Loren Coleman's contention that lions sighted in America are of the supposedly extinct American species, sightings have been made of maned lions in Nebraska, Ohio, Oklahoma, Washington, New Mexico and Arizona, but American lions are not supposed to have been maned. A maned lion was also seen in Kapuskasing (Ontario) in 1960. There is some doubt amongst scientists whether the American lion was a subspecies (*Panthera leo atrox*) or a species (*Panthera atrox*). However, the suggestion that it was actually a tiger is no longer upheld.

AMERICAN PTEROSAUR *Add to Dictionary article* Reports have continued to come in of creatures resembling pterosaurs in the United States. In 1968 or

1969 a number of these creatures were allegedly observed in North Ridgeville (Tennessee). The witness claimed there were about seven, perhaps nine, of them. In 1972 one was reported by truck driver R. Monteleone in Colorado. There have been a number of reports from Oregon, including one from some boys who saw this creature in the 1970s. In 1988 a flying creature larger than a pickup truck, its skin unfeathery but bat-like, was seen in Brookfield (Wisconsin) by a man staring out of a hospital window. In 1993 a couple saw a bird in a field near Orin (Wisconsin) It was a greeny grey colour and the head resembled a horse's somewhat, but seemed to taper into a beak. It had wings that looked like, but were not identical with, those of a bat. One witness put its length at 6', the other at 5'. In 2004 one was observed at Henderson (Kentucky). It was featherless, leathery and coloured red. Its wingspan was estimated at at least 30'. It had a kind of knob at the top of its head.The same year a pterodactyl-like creature was noted at Mesa (Colorado). The witness said it had no teeth in its beak. Reports have also come in from Utah, Michigan and New York. [BB]

AMERICAN TIGER *Add to Dictionary article* A beast thought to be a tiger killed a horse in MacDonough (Illinois) in 1891. Another tiger was reported in Nebraska in 1923. [A6]

ANEGADA SNAKE A small red snake was once reported from this, one of the British Virgin Islands, but it has not been seen since and its identity remains a mystery. [A6]

ANGUANE A wild woman of Italian folklore. Anguanes sometimes have feet like a goat's. They are sometimes a mixture of woman and snake. [155]

ANIMAL-FISH A strange creature allegedly landed by a fisherman in Nevada. It was 18" long, had hair, nine legs, a fin, gills and fish scales. It is described as neither animal nor fish, but looking like both. The report is dated 1905. [A6]

ANIMIKII Chippewa name for the thunderbird.

ANNISTOWN WILD MAN A wildman reported from Alabama in 1938 which seems to differ from your usual bigfoot.

Though completely hirsute, it was only about 5' tall and its face had a definitely human look about it. It was accompanied by a female and child. The being was said to roar like a lion. [A7]

ANTUKAI In American Indian lore, a gigantic sort of otter to be found in Oregon. [M]

AO AO In Guarani legend, this creature looks like a sheep with huge teeth or is a giant peccary. These creatures eat humans, but you can escape one by climbing a palm tree. [190]

APE-LIKE CREATURE In 1979 this was discovered by a couple in a car near Charters Towers, Australia. It was a metre tall. They described it as half man, half ape. [S11]

ARABHAR A kind of flying snake said to be found in the vicinity of the Arabian Sea.

ARABIAN BLOODSUCKER In Fujairah, United Arab Emirates, a bloodsucking creature has been reported attacking and killing sheep. A comparison with the chupacabras has been inevitable.

No description is to hand. [120]

ARIZONA FLYING SNAKE There
have been alleged sightings of flying snakes
in modern Arizona. They are also known in
Navaho and Hopi tradition, but the Hopi
snakes are supposed to be different from the
Navaho ones. A modern Hopi witness said
he saw what looked like a flaming flying
snake. [1]

ARKANSAS CREATURE Two of these
were seen together in 2006, about 3' at the
shoulder, with canine-type faces, long ears
reminiscent of a mule's, front legs longer
than back ones, chests massive and backs
sloping rearwards. [200]

ARLESFORD CAT ABC reported from
Hampshire in 2006. Its head was black, its
body chiefly off-white with brown marks.
The tail was black. The pointed shape of
the ears drew the witness's particular
comment. [F12]

ASIN In the beliefs of the Alsea Indians, a
female monster that abducts children and
other humans. [201]

ASPIS A medieval dragon, two legged and

sometimes wingless. [219]

ATAHSAIA Zuñi Indian name for a
BHM.

ATARA CREATURE A carcass washed
ashore in Egypt in 1950. It has never been
identified.

ATLANTIC SATYR According to
Pausanius, writing in the 2nd Century AD,
a ship was blown of course in the Atlantic.
The crew came to an island of tailed men or
satyrs. Their tails resembled horses' and
they were of an unfriendly disposition.

ATLAS DRAGON The writer Leo
Africanus (?1488-?1554) claimed dragons
were to be found in the Atlas Mountains of
North Africa. Large serpents, which may
have inspired the legend, have been found
in North Africa in modern times.

ATTERCROPPE A strange kind of snake
in German folklore. It is small in size, with
arms and legs like a human's. [M]

AUBURN BEAST A strange animal,
perhaps of the same species as the Turner
Beast, seen at Auburn (Maine) in 2004 by

L. Doyon. He asserted it was not a wolf, fisher or coydog.

AUSTRALIAN PIGMAN This was seen by an observer looking down from a clifftop. Its head was like a pig's, but turned upright. It had white axillary hair. It fought with a dog that died shortly afterwards. This incident was reported in 1878. [X]

AUSTRALOPITHECUS A form of ape generally regarded as an ancestor of the human race by scientists. It dwelt in Africa and is supposed to have become extinct a quarter of a million years ago; yet P.V. Tobias, an authority on the subject, had a colleague who believed in its possible continued existence and set traps to catch a specimen. Tarzan enthusiast Philip Jose farmer felt australopithecoi best conformed to the kind of apes that raised Tarzan in E.R. Burroughs' novels.

AVALERION A mythical bird supposed to be found in India. There were only ever two of them, a male and a female. Every sixty years they would lay a brace of eggs and drown themselves. [190]

AVON CREATURES The Avon Wildlife Area (Wisconsin) is said to contain an area where monsters exist. They were the results of genetic experiments by scientists, but eventually killed the scientists, so rumour would have us believe.

In 2003 some teenagers were chased by a strange bipedal creature in the area. It had a somewhat bushy tail.

Later that night they saw a bunch of similar creatures drinking (not lapping) from a stream. They showed some distinctly canine features, looking like dogs with human bodies. They also had tails. Their shoulders were broad and they had claws on their hands. [G12]

AWFUL, THE A large creature with greyish wings, each ten feet in length, spotted in the towns of Richford and Berkshire (Vermont) in 1925. The sight of it on a roof gave an onlooker a heart attack.

In 2006 a huge bird slaying a crow was observed by a horrified witness in Richford. Various sightings had been said to occur in the intervening years.

A supposed petrified partial jawbone of an Awful has been discovered.

Horror writer H.P. Lovecraft claimed the Awful had been one of his inspirations. [1]

BAA Huge bird of prey in Comanche lore. This is sometimes said to be a synonym for the thunderbird. [A6]

BABOON-LIKE CREATURE This was reported in Indiana in 1896. [A7]

BABOON-MAN A creature seen on Phillip Island (Victoria) about 1879. It was described as looking like half a man, half a baboon, with a rather long neck which appeared to be feathered. [X]

BABUSHKA-LYAGUSHKA-SKAKUSHKA In Russian legend, this was the oldest living creature. It was a frog which grew to the size of a horse. [D4]

BACA CREATURE Baca is in the San Luis Valley (Colorado). A couple have been seeing a creature 2'-3' in length. It appears to be see-through in parts and to taper at the ends. [224]

BACKAHASTEN In German legend, a sort of magical horse, often seen in foggy weather. Mount it and it will jump into the river with you. Such creatures seen in poor visibility with a tendency to jump into rivers when a rider climbs upon them are not confined to German folklore and one wonders if some horselike river creature may not lie behind the legends.

BAETYL *Add to Dictionary article*
Before we become too dismissive of stones' having a vital element, it is worth noting that some modern French geologists are contending that there is some kind of vital force within stones, that stones actually breathe (albeit very slowly) and that they can actually move themselves (over minute distances). Stones also experience the aging process. The French geologists said to have made these contentions are A. Rheshar and P. Escallot. [english.pravda.ru] With regard to living stones, Roman writer Licinius Mucianus, as quoted by Pliny, wrote of stones that ate corpses and gave birth to pebbles.

BAKENEKO A cat which has acquired supernatural powers in Japanese folklore. Its tail may sometimes develop into a fork, whereupon the animal is known as a nekomata.

BALZI ROSSI GIANT This creature is supposed to live in a cave in northern Italy.

In the 1940s a Russian surgeon, S. Voronoff (died 1951) living in this area was said to have tried to transplant gorilla testicles into humans. Could this be the offspring of one such human? [CERBI website]

BANBURY GIANT RABBIT Near Banbury, England, T. Hill and others saw a giant rabbit. They discounted kangaroo or wallaby identities. [#9]

BARMOUTH ANIMAL A creature seen in the bay of Barmouth in Wales. It had a head shaped like an egg, spines protruding from its back and an overall resemblance to a turtle. [146]

BARNES MOUNTAIN SABRETOOTH A sabretooth has been reported from Barnes Mountain (Arkansas). [2]

BASILISCO CHILOTE It has a cock's crest and a snake's body and lives under houses in Chile on a diet of human phlegm, which kills off those who live in the buildings. [190]

BASILISK *Add to Dictionary article*
Belief in the basilisk is also found amongst

the Hispanic population of the Rio Grande area. According to them, a hen gives birth to a basilisk viviparously, which must be a bit of a shock for her. Though they believe the basilisk's glance to be deadly, if a human sees it first, it will die. [200]

BASS LAKE MONSTER A monster in this Indiana lake was reported in 1881, when it destroyed the fishing net of a man named White. There were further reports, the last being in 1893. The animal had a pointed head and no fins. [N/S]

BASSETLAW BEAST Unidentified felid which left pawprints near Gainsborough in 1998.

BASTROP CREATURE A creature which looked like an armadillo, but was the size of a large dog, was reported at this Texas locale. [2]

BAYAMON CREATURE Its face was decorated with a nose like a snout, it was somewhat hunched and was generally humanoid in shape. It had long pointy ears. It was seen in Puerto Rico in 1998. [224]

BEAR-DOG This strange creature was

seen about half an hour's drive from Green Bay (Wisconsin). It looked like it combined features of bear and dog. It rose upon its hind legs and was 7'-8' tall. [2]

BEAR-MAN A creature seen in a wooded part of Pennsylvania in about 2007. It was described as bear-like with human features and it is alleged it attempted to talk. [2]

BEARWOLF A creature which seems to combine characteristics of bear and wolf, reported from Wisconsin. In the Antigo area it seems quite well known to the locals. [G12]

BEAST OF BALSHAM Legend says a large, black animal prowls this area of Cambridgeshire. It has in the past been described as looking like a dog or monkey. More recently, it has been thought to be feline. [1]

BEAST OF BERWICKSHIRE Large unidentified rodent resembling a guinea-pig, seen in this Scottish county. It is perhaps a capybara or coypu.

BEAST OF BESNAIS Mysterious French animal responsible for killings between

1693-5. [2]

BEAST OF BLADENBORO Bladenboro
(North Carolina) is a small town whose
current population is about 1700. In 1953-4
a dog-killing animal resembling a bear or
panther (=?puma) with a round face, over 4'
in length was said to be killing dogs in its
area. It was even described as a "vampire
beast". W.G. Fussell, the mayor, at some
stage claimed the animal was largely the
result of over-imagination, but he had
earlier helped to promulgate the story to
gain the town publicity. [200]

BEAST OF BRIVE A mystery predator
on the rampage in France in 1783. [2]

BEAST OF DEAN A large animal was
seen in the Forest of Dean, England, in
1807. Although the hunters had thought it
might be a boar, they could not identify it
with certainty when at last it was killed.
For two centuries nothing further of strange
animals was heard thereabouts. Then in
1998 two men were said to have been
chased in the area by a large beast the size
of a cow. This animal has also been called
a moose-pig. [190]

BEAST OF FUNEN ABC seen in Denmark from 1995. It was light yellow in colour. Some think it was a lion.

BEAST OF RIBER Mystery animal reported in Derbyshire, but there is doubt about even the category into which the animal fits.

BEAST OF SARLAT This mystery predator killed about thirty people in France in 1788. [2]

BEISHT KIONE Literally, 'beast of the head' (Manx). A black-headed sea monster which the Manx believed was to be found in the Irish Sea. [M]

BELGIAN MYSTERY CREATURE A large creature resembling a guinea-pig, seen in June, 2006. It may have been an out of place capybara. [2]

BENBROOK LAKE MONSTER An artificial lake in Texas, Benbrook Lake was constructed in the 20th Century. A witness called J. Lean reported seeing a monstrous form entering the lake. He described it as having dark fur. He said it stood upright, which I take to mean it was bipedal. It may have been 7-8' tall. [1]

BENNINGTON MONSTER A kind of hominid reported from the area of Glastenbury Mountain (Vermont). It was supposed to have overturned a stagecoach in the 19th Century, but has been reported as recently as 2003, indicating that a population of the creatures exists. The area of Glastenbury Mountain has a reputation for strangeness. Spook lights, phantoms and human disappearances have been recorded from there. Indians are said to have regarded the mountain as cursed. J. Trainer of *UFO Roundup* called the town of Glastenbury the paranormal capital of Vermont; but its population is only six. It is presumably called after Glastonbury in England, which is well known for its mystic associations. [C27]

BERRI ANIMAL This creature was seen in a tree in South Australia in 1954. Its scaly body was about 2m in length. The head seems to have been bizarre, but descriptions are lacking. [224]

BETHESDA CREATURE At about 10.30 p.m. on 20th July, 2005, near Bethesda (Tennessee), S. Nichols saw a strange creature. It was nearly 8' in height and seemed to be almost humanoid. The arms were joined to the knees by webbing. Most of the body was red. [244]

BETIKHAN In the lore of India, this creature had a human head and arms and the body of a deer. [M]

BICHA In Spanish lore, this creature had a man's head and a bull's body. [M]

BIELLESE WILDMAN According to Italian folklore, a wildman once lived in this vicinity. There is an indentation in a rock here called the *Sasso dell'Uomo Salvatico* (Wildman's Stone). [155]

BIG BUNNY Name used for phantom kangaroos in Coon Rapids (Minnesota) during a spate of sightings between 1957 and 1967.

BIG CYPRESS SWAMP MONSTER Name used for a BHM at Jefferson and Marshall (Texas).

BIG FISH Large and dangerous marine creature in Alaskan legend. [M]

BIG GREY CAT This creature was grey with darker body markings. The tail was thick. It was seen in Fife, Scotland, in 2002.

BIG HAIRY MAN A large hominid reported from Somerset County (NJ). It is said to be about 8' tall and to have a human stance. Its hair is the colour of a deer's. The beast seems to favour the Great Swamp as a hangout. [S20]

BIG-HEADED LLAMA This animal (*Hemiauchenia*) roved Florida nine million years ago. Although supposedly extinct, there was an alleged sighting in 1997. [2]

BIG RED EYE A large humanoid with glowing red eyes reported from Sussex County (NJ) It was supposed to be the utterer of a stream of nighttime wails that lasted for a fortnight in 1977. There have been several sightings, including a notable one in 1996. [S20]

BIG RIDEAU LAKE MONSTER A boating party saw a monstrous animal in this lake in Ontario about 1960. [79]

BIGFOOT *Add to Dictionary article* The

creature seems to thrive particularly in Oklahoma. C. Halmark recently estimated that the state harboured a population of 300, including family groups. A (human) family in Lost City claims to have been watching the creatures for three generations. Sightings have occurred in Eldon, Pumpkin Hollow, Welling Bridge and Hanobia, where a Bigfoot Festival has been held. It has also been suggested there is a population in western North Carolina. In the 20th Century there were 200 sightings reported in Maryland.

There has recently been a bigfoot hunt at Funks Grove (Illinois) where two witnesses had claimed a sighting, but it is doubtful if there is sufficient provender to sustain it in that area.

In January, 2006, a number of witnesses reported a big black hairy animal, not a bear, in Allegheny County (Pennsylvania).

Some books claim the only U.S. state with no bigfoot sightings is Rhode Island. However, there have been at least two sightings there of a white bigfoot (or white bigfoots), one in 1974 from near Wakefield and one in 1978.

Whitehall, NY, is a place where many bigfoot sightings are reported. They are also seen at times in the region of the

Hockomock Swamp (Mass.).

Don Avery, politician, reports he saw a bigfoot in the 2000s in the Liberty area of Washington state.

In 2007 a possible bigfoot footprint was found in Spotsylvania County (Virginia).

L. Coleman and P. Huyghe, who argue for the existence of different kinds of hominoid in North America, have suggested that these may sometimes crossbreed, producing hybrids, accounting for creatures like Momo and the Big Muddy Monster. M.A. Hall would identify the almas with *Homo erectus,* the Bushmen of Alaska and Canada with Neanderthals, true giants with gigantopithecus and the yeti possibly with dryopithecus.

At a controversial level, some would hold that bigfoots have a language. Albert Ostman, allegedly kidnapped by bigfoot, produced two bigfoot words - *soka* and *ook.* A man named Carter in Tennessee claims he taught a bigfoot named Fox to speak some English and his granddaughter alleged she had compiled a vocabulary of 223 bigfoot words and phrases, but others have treated this with caution. It is said bigfoots call humans *nenepe,* a pejorative term.

Pueblo Indians in the San Luis Valley

(Colorado) belief the Creator appears to humans as Bigfoot.

The term *blobsquatch* has appeared to designate any vague photograph of what might conceivably be a bigfoot. [197 C27 1 2 12 200]

BIGFOOT-HUMAN HYBRID There is a folktale in Tennessee which tells that a woman was once made pregnant by a bigfoot. She and her husband reared the child, but it did not respond as a human and eventually had to be trained to survive in the woods. The curious aspect is that it was absolutely hairless, which you would not expect of a creature with bigfoot genes. It is said it grew to 7'/8' in height. [154]

A writer named E. Fuchs in *Anthropologist* 1992 claimed he was told a Spokane Indian woman had been kidnapped by a bigfoot, but escaped, later giving birth to a hybrid son named Patrick, ugly but intelligent. Patrick married and had five children, at least one of whom was alive when Fuchs was told the story.

BIGHOOT Term invented by Mark A. Hall for a giant owl he believed to exist. He felt it could be the size of a man or larger.

BILI APE *Add to Dictionary article* This has now been identified as a subspecies of chimpanzee (*Pan troglodytes schweinfurthil*) with some distinctive features. [#9]

BILLY HOLLER BUGGER A term for a BHM used in Georgia. There was a notable sighting at Blackburn State Park in 1974. I have also come on references to this term being used for a BHM in Florida, but this may be due to confusion.

BINGBUFFER Type of lizard said to have been found in the Ozarks in American folklore. [R]

BIPEDAL CREATURE Strange unidentified creature said to have been photographed on a Florida farm. It looks mammalian to me, but I can discover no clue to the provenance of the photograph. [154]

BIPEDAL FOX A correspondent of the *Fortean Times* Message Board claims to have seen a fox, larger than a fox should be, walking on its hind legs.

BIRD OF KILCORNEY A bird in the folklore of Clare, Ireland, able to converse in human speech.

BIRD OF WASHINGTON *see* **Washington eagle.**

BIRD PEOPLE The second race to occupy the world, according to the Southern Sierra Miwok Indians. [S.A. Barret *Myths of the Southern Sierra Miwok,* 1919]

BIRDMAN A creature reported in West Virginia in the early 20th Century. [197] Do not confuse with the Birdman in *Cryptosup.*

BIXIE Winged cat with horns in Chinese lore. Their appearance indicated that the current government was good. They were supposed to keep away evil.

BLACK COUGAR According to standard zoology, there is not supposed to be a black form of the puma or cougar (*Panthera concolor*), but there have been reports of such animals from Kentucky, Nebraska, Tennessee and South America. If they in fact exist, they may account for black cat reports in North America. (There has been at least one supposed shooting of a black cougar in Brazil). Reports of these animals from Arizona are more likely, I feel, to be of black jaguars.

BLACK DRAGON This creature fell to earth in the ephemeral empire of Manchukuo (now in China) in 1944. It was described as having a horn and scales. The smell attendant on the dying animal was fishy. [#1]

BLACK FOREST CAT An unidentified felid which was in the Black Forest (Indiana) in 1877. It mauled one Mary Crane. [N/S]

BLACK SEA MERBEING Three of these were seen by underwater swimmer B. Borovikov off Anapa, Russia, in 1996. They were humanoid, large, white coloured and their tails were like those of fish. Large bulging eyes were described. One of them waved at the surprised Borovikov. [224]

BLACK-WINGED CREATURE In London in days agone, at the Old Chambers, Lincoln's Inn, astonished onlookers saw, through the window of his home, Charles Appleby fighting a bird-like creature which was shadowy. He was found dead the next morning. The doors and windows were locked from the inside. The bird continued to be seen for some time. [146]

BLESSIE A strange snake said to guard underwater treasure in a valley near Lindley (Free State), South Africa. Estimates of the length of this reptile vary from 15'-50'. Its colour is brown. [154]

BLUE CROW Large bird in the legends of Parana, Brazil. [190]

BLUE MAN OF SPRING CREEK This was said to be a purple-coloured humanoid which exceeded nine feet in height and was a feature of Missouri legend. It was apparently seen by a hunter named Collins in 1865 and seems to have worn moccasins. In 1911 its den was discovered, containing the remains of beasts it had eaten. The bunch of men who discovered it first saw it outside the cave mouth which formed its entrance. It retreated within, to be followed by a man named Alsop who discharged a shotgun, whereupon the Blue Man took flight, exiting by another egress. There was some speculation that the Blue Man had been a feral child. [A7]

BLUE MOUNTAIN DUCK *see* **Jamaica petrel.**

BLUE MOUNTAIN WARBLER A bird (*Sylvicola montana*) painted by Audubon, which has not been reported since, so its continued existence must be in doubt. [#9]

BLUE-BROWED FIG PARROT This parrot is known from only a single photograph, which, it has been suggested, is a fake. [B]

BLUFF ROAD MONSTER This creature is supposed to live in the Kettle Moraine near Palmyra, Wisconsin. Judy Wallemac had a sighting after 1970. Rochelle Klemp also claimed to have seen it and said , though it was bipedal, it was not human. [G12]

BLUISH-GREEN HUMANOID A creature whose hands were webbed and which had fins in lieu of feet was reported diving into the water off Pagai, Samoa. The sighting is undated. [154]

BOAR-CREATURE In 1950 two men

descended into a mine in California, having seen evidence of a fire there. They allege they came on a boar-like creature with human-like hands. It was trying to smash a skull against the cave wall. It chased the humans away. [224]

BOGEY OF CRADDOCK MARSH
Although its cries were heard and its footprints found, this creature, living on an island off the Virginia coast, has never been discovered, though it has been said to have been pursued for centuries. [A7]

BOGGY BOTTOM MONSTER
Humanoid creature, long the subject of legend in Oklahoma. Witness Jackie Marlow said it was reddish-brown with long legs. [200]

BOISE ANIMAL This creature was seen near Boise (Idaho). It looked like a hybrid of a dog and an hyena. It was too tall to be merely an hyena. It was black with brown spots. [2]

BOLINAS SEA SERPENT This was seen within a wave by artist Tom D'Onofrio, who estimated its length at 40'-50', in the latter half of the 20th Century off the

California coast. [1]

BOLOGNA DRAGON The naturalist
Aldrovandus claimed to have encountered
this in 1572.

BOOGER DOG A spotted dog, larger
than a cow. It was encountered in
McDonald County (Missouri).

BOOGER OWL A huge kind of owl
reported by settlers in North America. This
species would carry off animals. [197]

BOONVILLE CREATURE In 1937 the
Cypress Beach area of Indiana was troubled
by a beast which tended to howl and ripped
a dog apart. A Mrs Duff, who saw it,
thought it was an ape, but a "stranger" who
entered the *Hammond Times* office claimed
it was giant sloth which he and his uncle
had captured, perhaps in Mexico, from
which they had come. It had escaped near
Evansville. [A7]

BORACAY SEA SERPENT An animal
about 50m long with a head not noticeably
separate from its neck seen off this island in
the Philippines in 1983. The witness had a
degree in biology. [79]

BORNEO BEAST A new animal of unknown species photographed in Kalimantan, the Indonesian part of the island of Borneo, in 2005, by the World Wide Fund for Nature. A little larger than a domestic cat, it has red fur. Karl Shuker has suggested that the animal may be a known but extremely rare species, Hose's palm civet (*Diplogale hosei*).

BOROKA In Filipino lore, a child-eating woman with an eagle's wings and a horse's legs. [M]

BOTANY BAY GIANT According to an English handbill, one of three giants seen in Botany Bay, he became drunk upon rum and was brought to England, arriving in 1789. He appeared a somewhat docile creature. He had a long beard and claws. [X]

BOTTLE HOLLOW MONSTER Bottle Hollow was originally a ravine in Utah. In 1970 it was turned into a reservoir. The Ute Indians harbour a belief that gigantic serpents lurk in it. The legend has perhaps been reinforced by tales of strange lights entering and quitting the reservoir. [K11]

BOYD TOWN BEAST A carcass washed ashore at this Australian locale in 1912. Its head resembled a horse's and its overall length was 8'. [B9]

BRAINSUCKER A ferocious creature is Massachussetts folklore. It has been said to linger in woods near Chester, Russell and North Adams. Its face is doglike, its tail long and it has 6' vespertilian wings. Aggressive of habit, it will attack humans and animals. [2]

BRISTOL HUMANOID Hirsute creature of average human size seen in Bristol (Conn.) in 2005. The face was not seen. [224]

BRITISH LION *Add to Dictionary article* There have been several reports of lions roaming Britain in modern times. One was reported near Nottingham in 1976, there is an undated report from Devon and a lioness was reported from Hertfordshire in 1994. [H18]

BRITISH LYNX It has been suggested that lynxes have been deliberately introduced into Britain for hunting

purposes. Alleged sightings have been reported in Cumbria and Dorset, while possible sightings have been reported in Yorkshire and Devon. The *Guardian* (23rd March, 2006) carried a report of a lynx shot in Britain in 1991.
It has been suggested that the lynx never became entirely extinct in Scotland.

BRITISH TIGER Reports of tigers on the loose in Britain are not unknown. In 1999 one was seen in Hertfordshire and a forklift truck was attacked by one in Yorkshire. More recently, there have been at least two sightings of a tiger in the Church Fenton area of Yorkshire in 2005.

BROCSHEE Literally, 'fairy badger'. It would attack men and cattle until a saint chained it to the bottom of Rath Lake (Clare), Ireland. It was supposed to have been seen in 1931. [204]

BROOKFIELD CREATURE Hairy bipedal creature seen at Brookfield (Wisconsin) in 2000. It ran by jumping. A kangaroo identity was ruled out. It had a generally canine appearance. [G12]

BROOKLYN BATMAN A winged

human reported over Brooklyn (NY) in 1887. [211]

BROWN BIRD A large avian combining features of emu and heron. Specimens were seen in Illinois in June, 2006. A similar bird has been reported from Wisconsin. [2]

BROWN'S LAKE MONSTER Blue and green monster reported from this Wisconsin lake in 1876. [N]

BRUNEI HOMINID Footprints, possibly of a hominid, have been discovered in Andulau, a forested area in Labi, Brunei. They were discovered by Liew Kim San. Some of the locals think jinn are responsible. [BruneiDirect.com]

BUENOS AIRES DWARF Small black dwarf reported by the inhabitants of Buenos Aires in the Barrio Casilda area. It was covered with hair. I fear I have no further details.

BUJANGA Dragon or dragon-like creature of Malaysian belief. [M]

BUKAVAC Dangerous water beast of Serbian legend. It has gnarled horns and six legs. It would emerge from its watery habitat and kill humans. [190]

BULLITT COUNTY BIRD An unidentified bird, 4.5' to 5' tall, seen in a Kentucky field in 2005. Its head was feathered. It was coloured black on top, brown in front. [29]

BUNDABERG HUMANOID This was seen at Bundaberg (Queensland) by a reliable security guard. It was walking along the surf at the edge of the beach, was about 6' tall and was covered in green scales with webbed hands and feet. It had fins, one stretching from its forehead over its head and down its back, the others stretching from wrist to waist, clearly indicative of a water-dweller. The witness felt he was receiving a telepathic message from the humanoid telling him not to be fearful. It then swam away. The humanoid was in no way repellant; if anything, quite the opposite. [S11]

BUNDLE-LIKE CREATURE This strange creature was seen in Cuba in 1915. Two horsemen saw it and one fired his pistol (?revolver) at it. It advanced on them, growing as it approached, until it was almost the size of a horse. The men fled.

If this story be true (note elegant use of subjunctive) we have here a creature with mysterious powers of inflation, perhaps some kind of air sac. [224]

BURLAP MAN This creature, seen in 1993 in Wisconsin, carries the name from the fact that the witness at first took it to be dressed in burlap, a coarse canvas used in parts transatlantic. The creature was a muscular hominid, about 6' tall, with long doglike fur. It was seen in Wisconsin in 1993. [G12]

BURLINGTON CREATURE A creature reported in a tree about the year 2004 in Burlington (Iowa). It was seen at night. It had a head like a seahorse, a serpentine body, wings reminiscent of a bat's and a tail. It reminded the witness of a dragon. [1]

BURNS ROAD ANIMAL Unidentified, possibly apelike, being seen by fire chief V. Doerr in Florida 2000. Doerr suspects it was a man in a gorilla suit. [198]

BUSH WREN A New Zealand bird (*Xenicus longipes*) which is possibly, but not certainly, extinct It may be possible to find lingering groups.

CABALLO MARINO On Chiloé Island, Chile, local folklore features this animal. It is an ugly horse of considerable size with a golden mane. It is used by witches. [193]

CABBIT *Add to Dictionary article*
Sometimes Manx cats have weak spines. As their tails are either non-existent or vestigial and as their spines mean they have to hop on their back legs, people sometimes think they are hybrids of cats and rabbits.

CABIN CREATURE Some kind of unidentified creature that tried to force its way into a cabin in Missouri in 1997. Its attempts were noted by occupant C. Algood, but it was his cousin who actually saw the creature, looking in through a window. He said it was hairless, beady-eyed and equipped with sharp teeth. [154]

CABOT ISLAND CREATURES Two strange creatures observed standing at Cabot Island (Nova Scotia) in 1971. The exact location of the sighting was Bonavista Bay. The witnesses were two brothers aboard a boat. The creatures seem to have

been humanoid in appearance. About 4.5'
tall, they seemed also very broad. Their
ears were large and their heads bald. Facial
characteristics could not be discerned
because of the distance. They had short
arms and legs. [A5]

CADDO CRITTER A humanoid creature
reported from the vicinity of Caddo Lake
(Texas) in the 1970s. [154]

CAFRE A boar that walks on its hind legs
and can converse in human speech in
Filipino lore.   [M]

CAGUAS HUMANOID Illuminated
flying humanoid reported over Puerto Rico
in 2006. [224]

CAHORE SEA SERPENT Long sea
serpent seen off the Irish coast in 1976.
[B9]

CAJUN WEREWOLF This creature of
Louisiana folklore is said to differ from
other werewolves as it has canine or
vulpine parts. [214]

CALAMA CREATURE This was seen in
Chile in 2001. It was wingless, but flying.

The head was large. The body was over 1m in length. An additional report of what may have been the same creature came in three days later. [224]

CALIFORNIAN SEA SERPENT A 20'-30' serpent seen at the levy in Sacramento in 1999. [79]

CAMBODIAN STEGOSAUR A carving which much resembles, but cannot be said with any certainty to be, a stegosaur exists on the temple of Angkor Wat, Cambodia. This temple was dedicated between 1135-50, which would mean that the creature survived into historical times. [200]

CAMBRIDGESHIRE CAT A tortoiseshell ABC, grey and white in colour, was seen in February, 2005. There have been other sightings. [F12]

CAMPBELL LAKE MONSTER A monster was reported from this lake in South Dakota in 1934. The witness compared it to a dragon. Tracks indicated it had been ashore. [B9]

CAMPO RICO CREATURE A large-legged creature, generally humanoid in shape, with little wings to aid its propulsion, was seen here in Puerto Rico by a man named Perez in 1995. Later that night, a 5' creature was seen in the same area. [224]

CANNOCK CHASE HOMINID A large hairy biped reported from Staffordshire. A sighting by motorist Jackie Haughton, who described it as a large, hairy animal with glowing red eyes, occurred in 1995. A party of four saw it in 1998 and put its height at 6'8". The colour of the creature was described as 'blacky brown'. A further sighting was reported in 2004. D. Crawley of the Staffordshire Mammal Group was inclined to identify the animal as a big cat. A wolf-like creature, perhaps nothing more than a husky, has also been reported in the area. [12]

CAPE APE Name applied to BHMs by whites on the coast of Oregon.

CAPE COD JUMPER A humanoid that could make prodigious leaps and breathed blue fire, reported from Provincetown on Cape Cod (Mass.) in 1938. [224]

CAPE COD SEA-SERPENT This

boasted a long neck and two humps and was seen off Cape Cod in 2004. It was seen from 50/75 yards away, so the witnesses could see it clearly. [154]

CAPE LION A lion subspecies (*Panthera leo melanochaitus*) supposedly extinct since 1865. It had a black mane with a tawny area around the face. Some specimens have been rumoured to exist in South Africa, near the border with Lesotho. In addition, a possible specimen turned up in a Mozambique circus. [193 194]

CAPE MAY MONSTER A monster of elephantine proportions was washed up on the coast of New Jersey in 1921. Beyond the fact that it was a mammal, identification proved impossible. It was eventually carried out to sea. [S20]

CAPE TOWN CREATURE A correspondent of the unexplained-mysteries forum says that, around 2005, he was walking past an open drain when a huge unidentified shape, apparently able to change its form like liquid, shot from a tree into the drain, where it thrashed around showing strength. The drain was covered over quite promptly by the authorities.

CARBONATED SWAMP WARBLER
A bird (*Helinaia carbonata*) painted by
Audubon. It hasn't been seen since, so its
current existence is in doubt. [#9]

CARMEL SEA SERPENT Near the
mouth of the Carmel River (California) a
sea serpent about 40' long was discerned by
three men in 1948. It had hair which was of
a grey/green colour. [B9]

CARNIVOROUS VINE Allegedly
carnivorous plant, said to be found near
lake Nicaragua. In the *Illustrated London
News* in 1892 it is alleged a naturalist
named Dunstan had great difficulty in
freeing his dog from this plant. [225]

CASERTA MONSTER A most peculiar
monster reported from Italy in 1986. It had
long ears, was hairy and its eyes were
bright. It was seen in the mountains.
Overhead lights were sometimes observed.
[B9]

CAT MARA Name of a sea-monster of
Irish folklore.

CAT-FISH In medieval Europe it was

believed that this creature, which combined features of cat and fish, lived in the sea. [R]

CAT PEOPLE These occur in Louisiana folklore. They are supposed to be caused by Voodoo. [G12]

CATAZONON According to Aelian, a single-horned animal that fought with lions.

CATLIKE ANIMAL This unidentified creature was reported from the vicinity of Berkeley Township (Pa.) in 1979. [M12]

CATLIKE CREATURE 1 This large, unidentified animal was roaming around Upper Pottsgrove Township (Pa.) in 1973. [M12]
2 A creature about the size of a cat reported in New Jersey. It was allegedly seen in 2001. It looked like a cat with a primate's face and a tail which would remind one of a ferret. [2]

CEFFYL Y DWR *Add to Dictionary article* One Welsh legend says a water horse emerged from the River Towy. Its eyes were balls of fire and the breath it exuded was reminiscent of a furnace.

Another legend tells that a man hitched a water horse to his cart on the shores of Carmarthen Bay, but the animal dragged him into the water. [146]

CHAMBERS CREEK MONSTER
Name for a BHM used in the vicinity of Corsicana (Texas).

CHAMPAGNE-COLOURED CAT ABC reported in Essex in 1982. [154]

CHANAMEED In Pequot Indian belief, a hungry giant that also assaults women sexually. [201]

CHAPEL ST LEONARDS SEA CREATURE This creature, of which a head and two humps could be discerned, was seen in 1966 off the Lincolnshire coast. [146]

CHARLESTON BEAST In 1980 a black furry creature with a bushy tail and a lupine snout was seen near Charleston (WV). It proceeded on all fours, though stood on its hind legs when observed. It was then, according to the two witnesses, about 7' tall. [#1]

CHATEZ A beast half-man, half-goat in the folklore of the Balkans.

CHATS LAKE MONSTER This Canadian lake was said in days of yore to harbour a population of monsters. According to a report in an 1882 issue of the *Stevens Point Journal*, an actual specimen was killed by sailors. It proved to be 11' in length and 13" in circumference. [2]

CHAWAH In the folklore of Dominica, this is a kind of owl that can grow to gigantic proportions when a victim is near and seize it.

CHEERONEAR A class of dog-faced humanoid in Australian Aboriginal mythology. These creatures are to be found on the Nullabor Plain. Such legends may be the result of encountering small groups of humans disfigured by inbreeding.

CHEQUAH Potawatomi Indian name for a thunderbird.

CHESME A kind of blood-sucking cat spirit in Turkish folklore. [N. Jackson *Compleat Vampire*, 1995]

CHEVO MAN A goatman in California legend.

CHEVROUX HARNEAU GIANT A 9' tall humanoid observed at night in woods in 1913 in France. [224]

CHICK-CHARNEY Legendary bird of the Bahamas. It is reputedly the size of an emu and its beak looks quite menacing. [2]

CHI-LUNG A tricoloured Chinese dragon. Its colours are green, white and red. [219]

CHITAULI A species of reptoid in Zulu belief.

CHIAO A green dragon in Chinese lore. Its sides are yellow and its undeparts crimson. Its whiskers are reminiscent of those of a catfish. It has spines on its back and tail. It lives in mountains or swamps. [209]

CHILEAN FLYING CREATURE   In the early morning of 2nd August, 2001, a flying creature that looked horrible and was larger than a condor was sighted by a driver near Antofagasta. There had been other reports of such a creature. [224]

CHIPPING NORTON BEAST A beast with two heads and the wings of a bat was reported at this English locale in 1349.

CHORTI A BHM of Guatemalan lore. [M]

CHUPACABRAS *Add to Dictionary article* Reports of this creature have continued. An animal that looked like a crouching man-ape with a spiny back was seen in Tucson (Arizona) in 2003. A creature which seemed aggressive was reported in St John (Indiana) in 2004. A similar creature, but with the ability to fly, attacked pigs in the Dominican Republic in 2005. [154]

CIDRA CREATURE A strange winged creature was seen on a branch in this Puerto Rico locale in 1995/ [224]

CIGOUVE A hominid in Haitian belief. It has a human head, but a feline body. [201 R]

CIKAVAC Bird of Serbian folklore,

engendered by magic. [190]

CINNAMOLOGUS A bird which
collected cinnamon and brought it to
Arabia, according to Herodotus.

CLEVEDON SEA SERPENT In 1907 a
man in a boat was thrown overboard by a
serpentine creature which leaped out of the
water, but he managed to regain his vessel.
This happened off the Somerset coast.
[146]

CLIFTONVILLE SEA MONSTER A
creature with a horse's ears, seen off the
Kent coast in 1950. [146]

COJO Creature reported from a forest in
Belgium. There is little doubt that it is
canine, with slim legs and a burly body. Its
tail resembles a thylacine's and it has much
facial hair. [2]

COLO COLO A snake born from the egg
of a rooster that drinks the saliva of
sleeping humans. It features in the legends
of the Araucanian Indians. The Mapuche
Indians say it looks like a snake, the
Huillichas that it has a cock's head and a
mouse's body. [190 M]

COLORADO CREATURE Mystery bipedal creature whose three-toed footprints have been found in northern Colorado. It may also be responsible for unexplained noises. [2]

COLUMBIA CREATURES These have been reported jumping out in front of cars near Columbia (Pennsylvania). They are described as half fox, half cat. [225]

COLUNN GUN CHEANN This was a monster which once supposedly lived in Scotland and its Gaelic name indicates it was a body without a head. It was killed by one of the MacDonald clan.

CONVERSE CARNIVORE In Texas legend, a creature part wolf and part human. [G12]

CORNISH WHITE CAT An intensely white cat, bigger than a large dog, seen in Cornwall. [H18]

CORTEZ DINOSAUR There have been a number of reports of unidentified reptiles near Cortez (Colorado). A woman sighting one in 1996 averred it was 3'5" tall and of similar length. It had green/grey skin without markings. A similar creature had been seen near Dove Creek in 1966. Other sightings have occurred. One possible sighting was by motorists near Yellow Jacket. [A6]

COSTA MESA SEA SERPENT This creature was observed off California by a nearby surfer. It was likened to an eel. [B9]

CREATURE OF McCONE COUNTY Strange animal, perhaps but not certainly a wolf, killed in Montana in 2006. It had been responsible for the deaths of 120 livestock. DNA tests are now being conducted in an effort to identify it. [1]

CRETAN GIANT Ancient naturalists believed Crete had once harboured giants. They had found bones which were probably those of elephants.

CRIMEAN ANTHROPOIDS In the Crimea, Ukraine, three creatures were seen by campers in 2005. They resembled gigantic apes and seemed to have humps of some kind on their backs. They were covered in hair, but the fur on their eyebrows was light. [224]

CROSSWICKS REPTILE   It is said in tradition that, in the 19th Century at Crosswicks (Ohio), this lizard, which was 30'-40' long, captured a boy who was rescued by adults. The animal took refuge in a hollow tree, from which it was later flushed. It eventually escaped down a hillside hole. [A6]

CROW CANYON GORILLA   Name for a BHM reported from California.

CUCUY   A small humanoid which fulfils the rôle of a nursery bogey in Latin America.

CULEBRE   In the folklore of Asturias and Cantabria, a dragon or snake, of considerable length, winged and virtually invulnerable, except for its throat. It has a treasure-guarding function.

CYNOCEPHALUS   This term, meaning 'dog-headed one', is the ordinary Latin word for a baboon. However, dog-headed men have been the subject of belief at times. Thus the Roman Emperor Diocletian was supposed to have appointed one to his army. St Christopher was said to have had a dog's head until his baptism.

Aelian did not disparage the cynocephali, whom he placed in India. They were good people, who could not talk, but who understood human speech. Pliny placed them in Ethiopia, but India and Ethiopia were much confused in the Roman mind.

CYNOPROSOPUS Dog-headed dragon of medieval legend. [M]

DAHDAHWAT Monstrous beasts in Seneca Indian belief. [R]

DAHU This beast has been believed in by tourists since the 19th Century. It is supposed to occupy the Alps, Jura and, latterly, the Pyrenees. It is said to resemble a fox or deer. However, it is generally thought to have stemmed from a legpull by local guides.

DALLAS COUNTY MONSTER Alabama name for a BHM.

DARD This creature occurs in the lore of the Australian Aborigines. Its body is reptilian. It has a cat's head and a mane like a horse's. [M]

DARK-FURRED CREATURE Strange animal seen after nightfall in Wisconsin in 1941 by two youths on their way to Muscoda. [G12]

DARTMOOR APEMAN This creature was reportedly captured on Dartmoor (Devon) in 1948. It was brought to a hospital in a police van and three days later taken away, allegedly for examination. [#7]

DARTMOOR SHAPESHIFTER In 1961 the folklorist Ruth St Ledger-Grub was told that there were animals on the moor which were in fact shape shifters, despite their normal appearance. It appears that in local belief some are were-animals. [#7]

DARWIN MONSTER In 1955 there was a report that a sea monster, not shorter than 30m, was seen speeding across the harbour at Darwin, Australia. [S11]

DECATUR DOGMEN One night a couple in this Illinois city looked out to see four bipedal dogs perambulating down the street. They walked up to a house and proceeded to examine it from the outside, one even jumping on the roof. [G12]

DEER/HORSE CREATURE A strange creature reported from Georgia (USA). The witness saw it in the distance a number of times. It left tracks, the forelegs looking like those of a deer, the rear tracks looking like those of a horse. On one occasion it charged the witness, who noted it had antlers. [2]

DEER-SHEEP HYBRID An animal was born in Northumberland in 1963 and thought to be a cross between a deer and a sheep. Actually, it was probably only a sheep showing ancestral characteristics. [#12]

DEHOTOGOSGAYEH The Iroquois believe in this giant, one of whose sides is red, the other black. [201]

DELAWARE HOPPER Unidentified animal seen in Delaware in 1979. It proceeded at a hopping gait. [B9]

DEN-BLEIZ Breton name for a werewolf.

DEQUINCY ANIMAL Mysterious roadkill found at Dequincy (Louisiana) some years ago. It could not be identified.

DERIDDER ROADKILL *Add to Cryptosup article* DNA tests have shown the animal's mother was a dog, but have not shown conclusively the nature of the father.

DESCALSO In New Mexico human-like footprints, too large to have been made by humans, are ascribed to creatures named *descalsos*, 'those who are unshod'. [A6]

DEVIL MEN In 1540 the Spanish explorer Coronado was told by the Zuni Indians of these dwarf creatures with knives (?projections) upon their backs and a propensity to drink blood. [C28]

DHAKAN Fish-tailed giant serpent of Australian Aboriginal belief. [R]

DHARMAPURI PREDATOR A mystery beast killed sheep in this area of India in 2005. [12]

DHINNABARRADA Emu-footed humanoids of Australian Aboriginal belief. [R]

DIABLO Name applied to BHMs by

Hispanics in the USA. Spanish
diablo=devil.

DIAMOND ISLAND MONSTER This
creature looked like a ball of fire with a
face in it. It was seen on Diamond Island
near Hardin (Illinois) in 1885 by two boys.
In 1888 some adults opened fire on it with
no effect. The creature chased them away.
[210]

DIJIEN A gigantic spider in Seneca Indian
mythology.

DOCAT The alleged hybrid of a dog and a
cat. In *Cryptosup* I said an American
tabloid was claiming that such creatures
were to be found in the USA. Now Cassia
Aparecida de Souza, a Brazilian, has
claimed that her cat gave birth to six such
hybrids. A blood test could only find
evidence of canine elements in the animals.
[#9]

DOG-BEAR A strange animal, large in
size, said to combine elements of dog and
bear has been reported from Brookfield
(Connecticut). [2]

DOG EEL I am informed by Gary

Cunningham that this seems to be a synonym for Horse-Eel.

DON TOMAS LAGOON CREATURE
A reptile, not a snake, a metre and a half long, seen in this part of Argentina by two women in 2005. [*Inexplicata*]

DOUBLE-NOSED ANDEAN TIGER HOUND In 1913 Percy Fawcett saw this strange breed of dog with two noses. The "tiger" in its name means the jaguar, called *el tigre* in Latin America. It was seen again in 2005 by John Blashford-Snell in Beni, Bolivia. [#1]

DOVER DEMON *Add to Dictionary article:* There was an alleged subsequent sighting of the creature near the Xaverian Brothers School in Westwood (Mass.), an area contiguous with Dover. [200]

DIV Magical bird of Russian legend. [D4]

DRAGON TURTLE In Chinese belief, a turtle with the head of a dragon.

DRAGONEL A young dragon.

DRY FORK CANYON HUMANOIDS

These grey-white creatures chased a group of people at this Utah locale in 2003. [154]

DU PONT MONSTER Name for a BHM used in Seneca (Illinois).

DUBAI CREATURE An unidentified creature off the coast of Dubai which was inflicting wounds that bled profusely on hapless swimmers. This occurred in 2006. [1]

DUMP CREATURE *Add to Dictionary article* It has been mooted that this is a blue-eyed snake shedding its skin. [200]

DUNBAR SEA MONSTER This was seen off the Scottish coast in 1939. [146]

DUNKINSVILLE CREATURE A hairy or furry creature with long arms and a short tail, grey in colour, seen in Ohio in 1997. [224]

DUNROBIN SEA SERPENT A sea-serpent of considerable length was observed off the coast of this Scottish location in 1873. [146]

DUNVANT PREDATOR A mystery

animal that killed 300 chickens at Bevexe Fawr Farm, Dunvant (Glamorgan). Some of the victims simply died of fear. [F12]

DUSKY SOUND CREATURE This animal was the size of a cat, mousey in colour and with a bushy tail. It could not be identified by members of Captain Cook's crew, who saw it in New Zealand in 1773. [S11]

DUTCH HOMINID A creature described as an "ape-man" seen at night time on the edge of De Veluwezoom National Park in the Netherlands about 1984. The single witness said the creature was about 7.5' tall. [225]

DUVA Swahili name for the chemosit. This may have had some influence on the identification of the chemosit with the Nandi bear, as it is not dissimilar to Arabic *dob*, 'bear'.

DZEE-DZEE-BON-DA In Abenaki Indian tradition, a monster which is so repulsive, it frightens itself. Just how it manages to view itself, I have not discovered.

EACHY A humanoid of English legend. They dwelt in lakes, but it was not unknown for them to emerge. A supposed sighting of one emerging from Lake Windemere occurred in 1873, while one was said to have been seen coming out of Bassenthwaite Lake in 1903. Both lakes are in Cumbria. [190]

EAST PACIFIC BEAKED WHALE
This whale has been reported a number of times. The bulls are black or brown with a white saddle. The cows and calves have a somewhat brownish colour on the upper parts and are lighter on the underside. [N]

ECUADORIAN JUNGLE CAT A small, brown-coloured animal said to exist in this country and to hunt in groups.

ED CAREY ROAD BIRD The two witnesses described this creature, seen in 1976, as horrible. It had a bald head and a face reminiscent of a gorilla's. The road in question is in Texas. [BB]

EER-MOONAN The Australian Aborigines tell that these creatures were to be found in the Dreamtime. Their bodies were those of dogs, their heads those of porcupines and their feet those of women. [M]

EGYPTIAN DRAGON Prospeo Alpini (1553-1617) claimed dragons were to be found in Egypt in the 16th Century. The *Ymago Mundi* (1410) also claimed there were dragons in Egypt, from whose heads you might remove precious stones. Getting near enough to the dragon to this might, I suspect, have caused problems. [BB Z]

EL PESTIZO Shadowy black human-shaped creature that has reportedly attacked a number of people in Argentina. [224]

EL YUNQUE ENTITY 1 A creature with features of a large bat which seated itself on the bonnet of a car in the El Yinque district of Puerto Rico in 1995. [224]
2 A photograph of a creature was taken on Puerto Rico on 11th June, 2005, at about ten o'clock at night. The photograph, which shows a humanoid with a bizarre head, may be seen at iraap.org/rosales/2005.htm [224]

ELLETSVILLE CAT Dark yellow but unidentified felid seen in 2005 in Indiana. [N/S]

ELM GROVE PREDATOR A possible unknown animal seen at this Wisconsin locale in 2005, but it may have been nothing more than a black bear, as it was seen after nightfall. [G12]

ENDROP A kind of water horse in Romanian folklore. [M]

ENFIELD HORROR *Add to Dictionary article* Rick Rainbow of radio station WWKI and three companions saw it. They recorded the hissing sound it made. They said it was 5' tall, but stooped. Its colour was grey.   [T4]

ENGECO I have found this word listed as the name of an unknown primate, but in fact it occurs in the work of a 16th Century traveller and probably signifies a gorilla.

ENGLISH WILDCAT Though the wildcat (*Felis sylvestris*) persists in Scotland, it has long been supposed extinct in England. It died out in the south, we are told, in the 16th Century and the last one died in the north in 1849. However, well-known naturalist Trevor Beer claims he saw possible wildcats in the south in 1984. Possible specimens were also seen in

Exeter.

ENTRE RIOS CREATURE In this
region of Argentina, farmer Oscar
Resteinor had a strange creature hanging
about his home for about three weeks. It
had long yellowish hair, hands that
resembled claws and big feet. It was
eventually chased away. [*Inexplicata*]

ESKIMO CURLEW A bird (*Numenius
borealis*) which may be extinct, but is not
certainly so. They were found in Canada
and Alaska and migrated to Argentina,
where there was an unconfirmed report in
1990. [190]

ETHIOPIAN GIANT FOREST HOG
Though often reported, the existence of this
animal has not been established.

ETRUSCAN WILDMAN The Etruscans
lived in modern Tuscany and were
eventually absorbed by the Roman Empire.
Depicted on an Etruscan silver bowl, armed
with a club and stone, in the midst of a
hunting party, we find a wildman, giving
the impression that such creatures were not
unknown to the Etruscans.

EVERGLADES DINOSAUR Creature looking like a reptilian kangaroo, 50' in length, allegedly shot and killed by a hunter about 1900. [200]

EVINGTON CREATURE Strange red-eyed creature, with kangaroo-like legs, running but not hopping, about four foot in height, seen in Evington (Virginia) in 1996 or 1997. [154]

EXETER BAT A giant bat, 1.2m in length, reported from Exeter in 2000. [146]

EXTRATERRESTRIAL MICROBES Red particles fell in Kerala, India, in 2001. Now G. Louis, of Mahatma Gandhi University, argues that the showers, of which he has taken samples, may contain alien microbes. [2]

FALLS CITY FLYING MAN A man with a frightening face and wings with lights attached to them seen over this Nebraska town in 1956. His wingspan was about 15'. His eyes were blue. His skin appeared old and wrinkled. [218]

FATISMA HUMANO Term used in Chiapas, Mexico, for a BHM.

FEATHERED SERPENT In parts of Mexico, such a serpent is believed to inhabit a nearby cave. This may be a leftover from the time Mexican natives worshipped the god Quetzalcoatl, whose name means 'feathered serpent'.

FELTON GIANT RABBIT A gigantic rabbit the size of a deer, black and brown in colour, which has been wreaking havoc on allotments in this village in Northumberland. [211]

FENCE MONSTER Very late at night in May, 2006, this creature was espied in Illinois, climbing or attempting to climb a fence. It was 3'-4' tall, had a long head which may have resembled that of an hyena and dark hair. The sole witness said it may have been a primate of some sort. [200]

FENNVILLE CREATURE Creature looking like a werewolf reported from Michigan. [G12]

FINMAN *Add to Cryptosup article* Finmen were sufficiently close to humans to ply boats and to have a society. In summer they lived on the island of

Hildaland, generally invisible to, but occasionally seen by, mortalss. In the winter they lived in an (?undersea) city called Finfolkaheem. There seems to be a vague tradition of a sea battle with finfolk in which their king was killed.

The finmen seem in origin to have been a combination of the selkie and the Norse tales of the Lapps/Saami, to whom they referred as *Finnir* and to whom they ascribed magical powers. The people of Orkney believed that the finfolk had actual fins which they could disguise as clothing, but the Shetlanders did not share this belief. A mermaid was a finman's daughter. If she married a finman she would go through three seven year periods - one of ravishing beauty, one of human beauty and one of being an old crone. This did not happen if she married a human husband, which such mermaids often chose to do. She would then shed her tail. Whether the tail was actually part of her body or an overgarment was a matter of dispute.

Finfolk were much attracted by silver. If one were pursuing your boat, you could fling a silver coin at it, which it would pursue in preference to you.
[www.orkneyjar.com]

FINWIFE The female of the finman in the lore of the Orkneys and Shetlands.

FIORDLAND MOOSE *Add to Dictionary article:* It now seems highly probable that a population of moose exists in this area of New Zealand. In 2005, K. Tustin found some moose hair, positively identified as such by Trent University, in the vicinity. He had earlier discovered a set of moose antlers. [#9]

FIRE-CAUSING BIRD Huge birds with a wingspan of about 4m were said to have caused fires in San Juan, Puerto Rico, in the 1980s.

FISH LAKE ROAD CREATURE A bipedal creature that scared a repossession man in Michigan. It looked like a cross between a baboon and an hyena. The body was thick. It had big pointed ears. [G12]

FISHMEN OF INZIGMANIN In American folklore, these creatures were to be found on the border between North and South Carolina. They had scales, webbed hands and tails. They are now believed extinct. [195]

FLORIDA CREATURE A hominid about 4' tall, seen near Kissimmee (Fla.) in 1900. It had shaggy black hair and carried a stick. Some thought it might have been an Indian. [A7]

FLORIDA FLYING SNAKE There have been a number of reports of flying snakes from this state.

FLORIDA SEA CREATURE A creature allegedly seen to the south of Tampa Bay. It looked like a scaled or armoured seal. It was first observed in 2001. Two photographs are unconvincing of its existence. [200]

FLYING ANIMAL Seen in Puerto Rico over twenty years ago, this was a dark brown simian being. It was not large and landed on a roof before flying off. The two witnesses, a boy and his grandmother, thought it might be a genetic experiment. [154]

FLYING ELEPHANT *Add to Dictionary article* According to Thai belief, all elephants were once white and capable of flight.

FLYING REINDEER Reindeer of children's folklore which draw the sleigh of Santa Claus. They may first have appeared in the poem *Visit from St Nicholas* which appeared in the *Troy Sentinel* in 1823. There is some dispute over who penned the poem. The idea that the sleigh was drawn by reindeer may have owed something to the flying reindeer which pulled the sleigh of Old Man Winter in Finnish tradition or even to the flying goats which pulled the chariot of Thor.

FLYING SERPENT According to a *New York Times* article published in 1888, three females and later other witnesses saw a snake-like animal propelling itself through the air, apparently without the aid of wings, in Darlington County (South Carolina). [A6]

FORACAT A large cat of Irish legend. It was chained to the bottom of Doolough Lake (Clare). [204]

FOREST GROVE CREATURE In 1993, before the chupacabras outburst, an Oregon farmer surprised a small hairy figure that had apparently consumed a goat's inner organs. [224]

FORSTTEUFEL This was a wildman captured in Austria. Details are supplied by Gesner. The capture took place in the 16th Century.

FORT WILLIAM CAT An ABC which looked like a tiger with no tail and had no pupils in its eyes, seen in Scotland in 2001. [146]

FORTH SEA SERPENT 1 A black sea serpent seen by over a hundred onlookers in the Firth of Forth (Scotland) in 1873. [146] **2** A brown sea serpent with large eyes and a head resembling a horse's, seen in the Firth of Forth in 1939. [146]

FOX SERPENT A species of water monster said to occupy Lake Alumine in Chile by the Araucanians.

FRANKLIN COUNTY BIRD A huge creature whose wingspan was estimated at 20'. It was seen standing in a pond in Burke (NY) in 1973. The witness thought it had feathers. [230]

FREEPORT CREATURE A creature that looked like a shaggy brown llama with a wolf's head seen in Freeport (Illinois) in 2002. A similar sighting was made by the witness's mother about a week later. [G12]

FRESHWATER MERMAID These creatures were formerly believed to exist in bodies of water in England. They were said to be found in Cambridgeshire and Suffolk. They were supposed to be dangerous, with a tendency to drown the unwary. Such creatures are also to be found in European lore. Merbeings were said to be found in the Elbe, Saale and Danube. [W7 G9]

FROG MAN Strange creature with brownish/green skin, a hump on its chest and a head like half a circle. It was about 3.5' tall. It was chased by a couple of witnesses. This occurred in Juminda in Estonia in 1938. [224]

FROG-MONSTER In Micmac legend, a mythological creature that swallowed the world's water. It was killed by Glooscap and the water was restored. [190]

FUKU-RIU Japanese dragons, said to bring good luck. [219]

GABORCHEND A creature in Irish

mythology. In Old Irish, *gabor* could mean either a goat or a horse, so this creature had the head of one of these animals.

GALLIPOLIS CREATURE Animal seen crossing the road at night by Ricky Hamilton at Gallipolis (Ohio). Its head was like a cat's, it was about as long as an opossum and had the hunched characteristic of that animal. It also had some rough skin like an armadillo's. Writing in 2006, the witness said the incident had occurred a few years previously. [2]

GARAGE ROOF CREATURE Strange creature reported on a garage roof in North Hollywood (Ca.) by A. Carey, who saw it in December, 2005. He seems to argue that it was neither cat nor dog, but had characteristics of both. He is also sure it wasn't a puma. Its colour was grey and black. [154]

GARGOYLE-LIKE CREATURES Large-winged flying creatures reported over an alley in San Diego in 2002. [224]

GEEBELOWK Legendary giant owl amongst the First Nations of Eastern Canada. [197]

GELDEWESTS Giants of an amicable nature in the lore of the Coos Indians. They are fish eating. [201]

GENETIC HYBRIDS Hybrids of humans and apes and other creatures have been allegedly produced by *in vitro* fertilisation. It is asserted that surviving specimens have been destroyed. It has been said this has been going on in the United States since the 1970s and earlier. It has been averred that rabbit/human hybrids have been produced at Shanghai Second Medical University and allowed to survive for several days. [2]

GEORGIA DOGMAN This was seen by an undertaker in Georgia, USA, in 2005. It had a doglike face and ears, was over 6' tall, browny-black in colour, bipedal, muscular, with feet like a dog's only bigger. The witness had a second sighting, this time with a companion. Although it charged the witness, it fled on all fours when dogs were released. [G12]

GEORGIA GOATMAN There seem to be traditions of a goatman in Georgia, USA, in the region of Burnt Mountain, but information to hand is sparse. [200]

GEORGIA HOMINID The Georgia in question is the one in the USA, not the Caucasus. It looked like a human, bent forward, but with bovine hoofs and a short tail. [A7]

GETEMAN A goatman of Danish folklore. It jumps out from behind bushes and frightens virgins (an endangered species in Scandinavia). I am grateful to Dr Lars Thomas for drawing my attention to its existence.

GIANT AMERICAN CATFISH *Add to Dictionary article* Specimens are supposed to be found at Navajo Dam and Elephant Butte (New Mexico). [A6]

GIANT CAVE SPIDER These creatures have been reported from the Ozarks. [2]

GIANT DRAGONFLY These insects were observed at Cosmeston Lakes, Wales, by cryptozoologist Oll Lewis and others, about 2001. The wingspan was about 30cm, making them far larger than any known British dragonfly. Their colour was light brown.

GIANT EEL According to Cardinal d'Ailly (1351-1420), these gigantic monsters of the ocean could attain a length of 300'. [Z]

GIANT MONO HARE A kind of large silver lagomorph reported from the Mono Recesses and Bear Ridges (California). The ears of this creature are said to be as tall as a man's waist. One witness averred the animal was some kind of jackrabbit; a jackrabbit is, in fact, a kind of hare. [2]

GIANT RATTLESNAKE *Add to Dictionary article* Folklore in New Mexico deals with such a beast which at last took refuge in the Rio Grande. [A6]

GIANT TABBY CAT A tabby cat twice as big as a Labrador was reported from Dorchester in 2005. [F12]

GIANT WHITE BIRD This creature, with a wingspan perhaps in excess of 15', was seen by a 15-year old girl near Watson (Saskatchewan) in 2004. [2]

GIBBSTOWN CREATURE A creature with blood exuding from its face, seen by a boy gazing out of a window in Gibbstown

(NJ) in 1951. [224]

GIGIAT A kind of wildman who plays the flute in the folklore of Val Masino, Italy. [155]

GILIKANQO Alternative name for the tokoloshe.

GITCHIE GOOMIE MONSTER A creature seen by the roadside by motorists near Lake Superior in 1994. Its appearance was frightening and in somewhat resembled a kangaroo. It had glowing green eyes and struck one witness as deranged looking. [154]

GOATMAN *Add to Dictionary article* M.A. Hall would argue that this creature is in reality a small ape.

GODLEY GREEN ANIMAL A strange animal reported from Cheshire, perhaps a ghost. It is sometimes said to be doglike, sometimes catlike and once it was identified as a lion. [H18]

GOLDEN BEAR A possible new species of the moon bear, with a golden coat, black mane and black rings around the eyes. A captive specimen was reported from Yunnan and another specimen was seen in Cambodia, which may be home to the species. [*Animals Magazine*]

GOLDSBOROUGH GROWLER A mystery creature of Queensland which seems to be known only from the growls it utters. Raids on farm animals have been ascribed to it. [1]

GOLLYGOG An animal in the folklore of the United States. It is supposed to have been in the Ozarks in the 19th Century. [R]

GOOD HOOP Term used in Tasmania to designate the bunyip (*see Dictionary*).

GORLESTON CREATURE A possibly paranormal creature, described as looking like a dog, but its legs were too long. It was seen twice by a woman in this Norfolk location, the second sighting being in 2006. [1]

GOURD HEAD A 3' tall creature reported from South America. It dwells in water and has a head shaped like a gourd and webbed hands. [195]

GRAVEDIGGER *see* **Kentucky Cryptid.**

GREAT CUMBRAE CREATURE Great Cumbrae is one of the Shetland Islands. In 1911 a strange creature was seen off the shore, with a head like a camel's and a neck like a giraffe's. [146]

GREAT ELK Huge wapiti of Apache legend, killed by the hero Djo-na-ai'-yi-in. [221]

GREAT HORNED SNAKE A large snake 10m long in the beliefs of the Kubu of Indonesia. They claim that these beasts are horned. Moreover, they aver that the snakes ultimately turn into huge crocodiles. This legend has apparently grown up because the Indo-Pacific crocodile (*Crocodylus porosus*) is to be found in the area. [#9]

GREAT LAKE MONSTER This Swedish lake near Ostersund is said to have been the location of monster sightings for over three hundred years. The animal has been variously compared with a horse and an eel. [1]

GREAT MEADOWS REPTOID This was seen in New Jersey in 1974. It was very tall and covered in green scales, yet it had a generally humanoid figure with batrachian eyes. [S20]

GREAT SALT LAKE WHALE In 1890 there was a report that a number of whales were to be found in the Great Salt Lake (Utah). It is, however, unlikely to be true for reasons of a non-conducive environment.

GREAT WITLEY CAT A large animal, twice as big as a tom-cat, killed in Worcestershire in 1962. It did not look like a domestic and the person who killed it was convinced it was a wildcat (*Felis sylvestris*), though this species has long been held extinct in England. [F12]

GREEN BANK CREATURE This was seen in a blueberry field in New Jersey in 1968. There seems to be no accompanying description. [M12]

GREEN HUMANOID Two of these, covered in hair, were seen by American golfers in New Zealand in 1989. [224]

GREEN'S FARM BEAST A farm at Florida (NY), property of a man named Green, boasts a cave which is said to be tenanted by a beast 8' high which attacks farm animals.

GREY-HEADED BLACKBIRD A bird (*Turdus poliocephalus*), also known as the Norfolk Island thrush, which is supposedly extinct. Yet a specimen was reported from New Zealand on the website *Cryptozoology.com*

GREY MAN Name used for a BHM in the Carolinas by whites.

GREY TENTACLED CREATURE This animal was seen crossing the road in Ohio in 1958 and was shortly afterwards discerned across the Kentucky border. It was bald and endowed with rolls of fat. [200]

GRIFFIN *Add to Dictionary article* The term *keythong* has been used in heraldry to denote a male griffin.

In the 16th Century, Toribio Motolinia had heard of griffins in Mexico, while the chronicler Oviedo claimed to have seen a small harmless one in Peru. He wasn't altogether sure it was a griffin, for he claimed it looked like the hybrid of a bird and a cat. [Z]

GRIFFY LAKE CAT Large felid reported from Indiana in 2005. It may have been a puma, but one commentator said its tracks were too large. [N/S]

GUARDIAN OF THE FISHES A huge freshwater fish of Estonian folklore. It guards the other fishes, attacking fishermen. It can even walk on land, where it sports human legs. [M]

GUBRI MAN In Australian Aboriginal legend of the Katoomba region, a humanoid monster with a large head.

GULON Large gluttonous creature in European mythology, having a dog's body, a cat's ears and a fox's tail. The animal behind the legend would appear to be the wolverine (*Gulo gulo*).

GWAGWAKHWALANOOKSIWEY Gigantic raven in the beliefs of the Kwakiutl Indians. [M]

HAETE A strange creature from Korean

legend. It is supposedly formed from stone and has advanced neophobia. Statues of the creature are found in Korean architecture.

HAIIT A humanoid creature with a small tail and three toes per foot which figured in 16th Century travellers' tales. It was supposed to live in Africa and rumoured to subsist on a diet of air. [R]

HAIKUR Water-dwelling creature of Icelandic folklore. It has been compared with the Scottish kelpie. [M]

HAIRY HUMANOID It was about 5' tall and seen near Hemat (Ca.) in 1993. [224]

HAKENMANN Human-headed fish said to live off the coast of Germany. [M]

HALF-MAN A half-man, half-ape reported from the Hockomock Swamp in Massachussetts. The witness did not call it a bigfoot, though it is said such creatures are to be found in the swamp. [200]

HANNO'S GORILLAS About the year 500 BC, a Carthaginian voyager named Hanno (Punic *Annon*) set out to set up colonies on the west coast of Africa, largely unknown to the Mediterranean world. We have an account of his voyage in Greek, based on a translation from Punic. He sailed as far south as a mountain called *Theon ochena*, which some would identify as Mount Cameroun, but is more likely to have been Mount Kakulima in Sierra Leone. Three days later they came to an island inhabited by wild people, whom their interpreters dubbed 'gorillas'. The men fled and they killed and flayed three females, whose skins they brought back to Carthage.

That they were not the creatures we call gorillas today is certain. One suggestion is that they were agogwe (see *Dictionary*), but there is no indication that they were diminutive. One wonders if they were a lingering population of *Homo ergaster*.

HANKE-WASICHUN Claims have been made that bigfoots speak an actual language and that, in that language, this is the name of a bigfoot-human hybrid.

HANTU BOJOR A simian creature of Malaysian folklore, smaller than a human. It is not as hairy as the hantu semawa. [1]

HANTU HUTAN Alternative name for the mawas.

HANTU SEMAWA A creature in the folklore of the Orang Asli tribe of Johor. It is apelike and of roughly human size. Do not confuse with the larger mawas. [1]

HARE CAT The supposed hybrid of a cat and a hare, dismissed as genetically impossible.

HARPY In Greek mythology, harpies were originally beautiful winged women. In later mythology they became winged hags. In medieval heraldry they were known as virgin-eagles.

HARRINGTON BEAST This animal, black in colour, was observed in Delaware in 1984. Although unidentified, it was a possible ABC. [B9]

HAVFINE Norwegian term for a mermaid.

HAVFRUE Danish term for a mermaid.

HAVHEST In Scandinavia, this creature had the head of a horse and the body of a fish or serpent. There was a supposed sighting in 1750. [M R]

HAVSTRAMBE A sort of merman in the folklore of Greenland, it has green hair and a beard. [R]

HAWAII GARGOYLE A strange creature that was hairy, had wings and huge claws, which succeeded in sucking all the interior organs out of pigs, but it seems to have made only hole-like punctures in the animals' necks. The witness saw the creature again some time later. [154]

HAYMAN LAKE MONSTER A monster is said to dwell in this Saskatchewan lake. It is perhaps serpentine. [N]

HERM MONSTER A creature with a long neck seen off the coast of Herm, one of the Channel Islands, in 1923. These Channel Islands are the British-ruled ones in the English Channel, not the ones off the coast of California. [155]

HERMANUS SEA MONSTER A sea monster seen not far from the South African coast in 1903. [B9]

HIGH-BEHIND In the folklore of the Ozarks, a lizard the size of a bull. Its back legs are longer than its forelegs. It generally conceals itself behind objects. It was possibly invented by settlers to stop their children wandering into the wilderness. Although the name is humorous, there are various stories of giant lizards in Ozark folklore and it may represent a genuine tradition of encounters with such creatures. [2]

HIINTCABIIT Huge water-dwelling horned serpent in the beliefs of the Arapaho Indians. [M]

HILA Alternative name for the tokoloshe.

HINTHAR In Burmese tradition, a kind of duck.

HOCKOMOCK BIRD A mystery bird reported since 1971 from the Hockomock Swamp in Massachussetts. It has an 8'-12' wingspan. It is black and looks like a creature from prehistory. [2]

HOGA Lake monster of Mexican folklore. It had a head resembling a pig's. It also had a tendency to change colour. It has been identified with a beast called andura in South American legend. [M R]

HOGANSVILLE BIRD A 3.5' tall bird seen in Georgia in 1994 by a married couple. Its wingspan was estimated at 10'. The bird flew into nearby woods. [224]

HOG-KILLING VARMINT In 1948 this creature was reported by farmers in Indiana. It was also seen by police officer L. Daniels, who said it was like something out of a horror film. It had long legs, a big head with pointed ears and small eyes. [1]

HOHOQ Kwakiutl Indian name for the thunderbird.

HOLLAND APE Ape seen in a car park at Holland (Lincs) about 1984. [230]

HOMME-PAPILLON, HOMME-PHALÈNE French terms for Mothman.

HONDO BIRD This unidentified bird was seen at night in 1983. It was huge and obscured the moon overhead. [BB]

HOOFED HORROR Creature in the folklore of Bangor (Maine). I would welcome any further information on this creature.

HOOK HEAD SEA SERPENT This animal was seen off the Irish coast in 1975. It was estimated at 20' and looked like a large lizard. [B9]

HOORI WOMAN The female of the Gubri Man. Her voice is frightening.

HOPPING DEVIL This creature was seen in West Orange (NJ) in 1924. Its mode of progress resembled that of a rabbit. Its head was like a deer's and it had fiery eyes. Witnesses included a policeman and a farmer. [S20]

HORN POND SHARK A large red fish which seems to be a shark has been reported from this freshwater lake in Massachussetts. [2]

HORNED ALLIGATOR Mystery reptile of Kiowa legend. [M]

HORSE-DEER HYBRID The supposed hybrid of a New Forest pony and a red deer existed in 19th Century England. It is most unlikely to have been anything of the sort. [#12]

HOTU-POKU A gigantic monster of
Maori lore. It looked like a large lizard. It
had many spines and great strength, but was
eventually trapped in a net. There seems to
have been only a single specimen, but it
belonged to the category of the Taniwha.
[R]

HOUKOU In Japanese folklore, a
paranormal dog that lives in trees. It has
five tails and, when it wags them all, it can
cause earthquakes.

HOUSTON CAT Mystery felid, only the
back end visible, observed 'some years ago'
in Texas. It was the size of a small puma,
but the tail was striped. [2]

HOY SEA SERPENT Off Hoy, one of the
Orkney Islands, in 1919 a long-necked
creature was reported. The said neck was
as thick as an elephant's foreleg. [208]

HULI JING Supernatural fox in Chinese
myth capable of turning into a beautiful
maiden. The term is sometimes used
pejoratively for a woman in modern
Chinese.

HUMA A bird resembling the phoenix in

Iranian mythology, half male, half female.
It burns itself to death from time to time,
but arises from the ashes.

HUMAN SNAKE These creatures, of
Seminole mythology, were snakes that
could assume human form. [R]

HUMAN-APE HYBRID A creature
which some speculate is a human-ape
hybrid called Bassou has been living near
Skoura, Morocco, for at least twenty-five
years. His facial features have some
distinctly simian qualities, while his arms
are so long his fingers hang below his
knees. He cannot talk. He eats dates,
berries and insects. [217]

HUMAN-OX HYBRID Giraldus
Cambrensis, writing in the 12th
Century, said that such creatures existed in
Ireland. One of them, to be found in
Wicklow, looked human except for having
bovine hooves, no nose and a bald head. It
had large eyes like an ox and could not talk,
but only low like a cow. A similar creature,
Giraldus claims, was born in the mountains
of Glendalough, the hybrid of a man and a
cow.

HUNTSVILLE CREATURE A short, hairy creature with a reptilian head was seen in a graveyard in Huntsville (Utah) in 2005. It gave off an odour like bleach. [189]

HYDRUS In the Graeco-Roman world, this creature was supposed to be found in the Nile, but there was some confusion about what it looked like. It was said to have had three heads. Isidore of Seville called it the *enhydrus*. In the Middle Ages it became somewhat confused with the ichneumon. Pliny thought it was an otter.

HYENA-LIKE CREATURE There have been several reports of these animals from the Ozarks. In one case, one of the beasts treed a hunter. [G12]

IARIYIN Hare Indian name for a BHM.

IHUAIVULU Seven-headed South American dragon that lives in volcanoes.

II Ocean-dwelling dragon of Chinese lore. [209]

IKO-TURSO A fearsome sea monster of Finnish mythology.

ILLINOIS BIRD Witness Joni Growe in 1977 saw three giant birds (two adults and a young). They were grey. The adults were of human size and they had feathered heads.

ILLINOIS CREATURE This was seen about 1989 at night in Naperville. The creature was bald, 3'-4' tall and clawed. The witness did not linger. [193]

ILLINOIS GARGOYLE This creature was said to have been seen in Elmhurst in 1981 by teenagers, who described it as a gargoyle. It had golden horns, a muscular body and arms, wings and leathery skin.

ILOMBA A sea serpent in which the Lozi of Zambia believe. [190]

IMPERIAL WOODPECKER A Mexican bird (*Canpephilus imperialis*) which may now be extinct, but this is not certain.

INDACINGA A BHM in Ponca Indian lore. It tends to howl in the manner of an owl. [201]

INDAVA Unknown flying creature of Papua-New Guinea, possibly identical with the ropen.

INDIANA PREDATOR Unidentified pig-slaying animal active near Fortune City in 1948. [N/S]

INDIANA VARMINT An unknown big cat seen in Indiana in 1948. It was described by a police witness as big-headed with long front legs. [N/S]

INE NARMIN In Mordvin mythology, a great bird that sits atop the world tree.

INJUN DEVIL A term used in Maine for various creatures, including the Eastern Bigfoot, but because of its wide and inexact application it should be deleted from the cryptozoologist's terminology. [200]

INVULCHE A monster of Chilean lore that resembles a bladder and dwells perpetually in a cave. If you wish to discover it, the way in is through a tunnel under a lake. It has vampiric tendencies. [M]

IOWA CREATURE A strange creature

which showed characteristics of a bear or a wolverine, neither of which is to be found in Iowa. [2]

IOWA DRAGON This was observed at night by a couple in Burlington (Iowa). It was coloured brown, had bat-like wings and resembled a Chinese dragon. Its body was about 10' long. The incident is undated. [154]

IOWA FLYING SNAKE A man named Corner saw this in Taylor County in 1887, at first mistaking it for a buzzard. It was large with protruding eyes and landed in a cornfield. [A6]

IQUIQUE CREATURE An unknown animal seen by a janitor on a Chilean rooftop. Its eyes bulged, its ears were long and its teeth looked far from reassuring. It had vespertilian wings and was about 1m long. [224]

IRISH GOATMAN This Pan-like figure was seen one night near Ballinahinch. It was Midsummer Eve. [#9]

IRISH WILDMAN According to a Norse work *Kongs Skuggsjo* (13th Century) a wildman was discovered in Ireland. It could not speak and had a mane running down its back.

ISLAND LAKE MONSTER This creature, 60'-70' long, was observed in this Michigan lake in 1955. [B9]

ITTIDU-BIRD An unidentified bird mentioned in a Sumerian poem. What it was is not certain, as Sumerian scholars have not managed to translate the word. The poem says it is not to be found in the paradise of Dilmun. The term *Dilmun* was applied to Bahrain, but may not mean that island in this case. As the ittidu-bird is mentioned along with the raven, it may be a carrion bird.

IYA Monster of Sioux Indian belief. It is noted for its halitosis. [R]

JABBERWOCK A creature invented by Lewis Carroll for a poem in his book *Through the Looking-Glass* (1872). The name was applied to a large hominid reported from Fresno (Ca.) in 1893. It was also used for some creature seen in Ohio a decade earlier. [A7]

JACKSON DRAGON A reptilian monster which attacked a farmer named Rishal near Jackson Township (Indiana) in 1879. In the course of the pursuit, the creature impaled itself on a reaping machine. Although the animal was to a degree serpentine, it was not identified as a serpent *per se* by those who found it. It had appendages described as tentacles or horns above each eye. [N/S]

JAGISHO Alternative name for the Great Naked Bear. See article in *Cryptosup.*

JAMAICA PETREL A bird (*Pterodroma carribbata*) last seen in 1879. However, it may still exist on the islands of Dominica and Guadeloupe.

JAVAN EAGLE Supposedly extinct eagle (*Spizaetus bartelsi*) allegedly seen in Indonesia in 1997.

JEFF Swedish name for the gulon.

JEFFERSON WINGED CREATURE A tall, generally humanoid creature with leathery wings and a non-humanoid face seen on the edge of Jefferson Marsh (Wisconsin) in 2005. [G12]

JENTILLAK Giants of Basque lore. The last of them was said to be a fierce and unpleasant character called Olentzero. However, in modern folklore Olentzaro has been turned into a Christmas gift giver of the Santa Claus type.

JENU Micmac Indian name for an anthropophagous BHM.

JILIN DRAGON A red object that appeared to be a dragon was seen in the sky by students at Jilin University, China, in 2005. A cellphone photograph was taken at the time. [#1]

JIMPLICUTE A creature in Ozark folklore, reported from Arkansas in the 1880s. It was said to resemble a dinosaur. It sucked its victims' blood. [2]

JOPLIN HUMANOID A thin, bald-headed creature, skin perhaps suffering from a xerotic condition, with big eyes, of short stature, seen in daylight in Missouri in 1993. [224]

JURIK Flying fire-breathing reptile of Indonesian legend.

KANENAREE A mythical bird of Myanmar, with a human head and hands. The female is called a *kanenayar.*

KANG ADMI Alternative name for the yeti.

KANGAROO-LIKE CREATURE A strange creature seen about 1997 near Dartmouth (Mass.). It resembled a kangaroo, but its eyes were bigger and its tail was fluffier. There were two witnesses. [2]

KAP DWA A huge stuffed giant exhibited in England. Although almost certainly a fake, an examination by two doctors and a radiologist could find no evidence that this was the case and suggested that it was a case of conjoined twins. It was still being exhibited in the 1960s and F. Adey, who thought it a fake, had to admit he could find no signs of joinings or stitchings together. It was said to have been of Patagonian provenance, but this may only have been because Patagonia had a reputation for producing giants. The giant was black, It has been said the giant was ultimately taken to the United States and ended up in New

Jersey. It has also been alleged that the giant was to be found in Newcastle-upon-Tyne in 1999. [#9]

KAR In Zoroastrian mythology, a fish resembling a serpent.

KARAU The Yupa Indians, who dwell in Colombia and Peru, believe in this creature which is a hairy hominoid with large teeth. They regard it as a spirit of the night. [212]

KARKAGHNE A creature supposedly to be found in the Ozarks, variously described as a diminutive humanoid or a BHM. Karkaghnes are said to be able to distend time, to make a traveller's journey seem longer. There is a Karkaghne Section of the Ozark Trail (Missouri). [2]

KARURA This fierce creature of Japanese mythology is a version of the Indian garuda (*see Dictionary*). It has an eagle's face (or beak) and a human body. It will attack dragons. [190]

KASHEHOTAPOLO In Choctaw lore, a primate which seems to have a somewhat misshapen head.

KATCHEETOHUSKW A large monster in the traditions of the Naskapi Indians. Its description may preserve a memory of the mammoth or mastodon.

KAWEKAWEAU Large lizard of New Zealand lore, said to be able to grow as large as 6'. It has been suggested it is a kind of gecko. According to tradition, its coat was brownish with red stripes. A stuffed gecko found in a Marseilles museum is, it is conjectured, a specimen of this animal.

KEMPER COUNTY CREATURE A fearsome animal in the folklore of Kemper County (Mississippi). There seem to be no descriptions of it, but its existence was inferred from noises heard in woods, etc. [1]

KENTUCKY CREATURE An animal seen near Louisville. It proceeded by leaping almost, but not exactly, on all fours. It resembled a mixture of a pit-bull terrier and a large wingless bird. [1]

KENTUCKY CRYPTID An animal seen by a witness on the way to Shelby City (now Junction City) about 1970. It jumped down ahead of him and seemed unable to see him. He conjectured this creature only went out after dark. Its face was somewhat like a bat's, its body was furry, it lacked shoulders and its arms, which were not hairy, seemed to stick out from its chest. The witness did not see its legs, but, when he made a noise, the animal took off, jumping a fence, implying that its lower limbs were powerful. This happened beside a railroad, near a graveyard. A second witness told the first he had seen a similar creature, also near a graveyard. The first witness speculated it might have been a creature in the folklore of his grandmother's generation, to which she had referred as a gravedigger. [209]

KENTUCKY GIANT DEER A creature which the witness saw in Kentucky in 1987 and which he tentatively identified as a deer. It had a thick mane and no antlers and was the size of a small horse. Its colour was brown/red, the former predominating. It resembled a wapiti. [2]

KENTUCKY GOATMAN A humanoid with horns and goat legs reported in Smith Mills (Kentucky) in the 1970s. [209]

KENTUCKY HYENA Creatures that are or resemble hyenas have been reported from this American state. One seen in 2004 was reported to have bluish-grey fur, black spots, a snout and long teeth. One seen in 2006 was said to be brown with black patches.

KENTUCKY LIZARDMAN A creature seen by a small boy looking through windows in the depths of the night in 1966 in Stephensport. It was bipedal, 5'6"-6' tall, with webbed hands and feet. [209]

KING LAKE MONSTER A creature reported in this Indiana lake in 1894. [N/S]

KINGDOODLE In Ozark folklore, a 5' tall lizard. It makes a booming noise. [2]

KIPUMBUBU Gigantic form of crocodile reported from Tanzania.

KIRNI A bird not unlike a griffin in Japanese belief. [R]

KNOBBY BHM reported from Cleveland County (North Carolina).

KO-GOK Monster in Abenaki Indian

legend.

KOKAKO *see* **South Island kokako.**

KOLOWOSI Gigantic water serpent of Zuni Mythology.

KUIGON A monster similar to and perhaps identical with the hibagon of Japan. [B9]

KUMI Large lizard in the lore of New Zealand. No sightings have been reported since the 19th Century.

KUN A huge fish in Chinese lore, supposed to live in northern waters. It can turn into a bird. [190]

KURUMBA SEA SERPENT A sea serpent with astonishing colouration. It was yellow/brown with blotches of blue, green and yellow covering it. It was seen from the ship *Kurumba* off Western Australia in 1939. [S11]

KWAKIUTL BIRDS Large birds in which the Kwakiutl Indians believed. The male was called Bakbakwakanooksiwac and the female Galokwudzuwis. [M]

KW-UHNX-WA Nootka Indian name for the thunderbird.

LA CIENGA CREATURE Creature seen in 2002 at night on a patio in Panama. It was a hominid, had dark ears that covered much of its face and its legs resembled those of a kangaroo. [224]

LA TURBALLE SEA MONSTER Seen off the French coast, this creature had a head reminiscent of a dog's and a long neck. [155]

LABELLE CREATURE This creature was seen in Labelle (Florida) in 1999. It was 3'-4' tall, with spikes on its back and disproportionately small arms. The witness was inclined to identify it with a chupacabras, but here caution is indicated. [154]

LACROSSE LIZARD MAN Bipedal creature with scales seen by two witnesses at this Wisconsin locale in 1993 or 1994.

LAGO BLANCO MONSTER Large reptilian creature reported in this Chilean lake. [1]

LAGUNA DON TOMAS CREATURE
A strange creature that looked like a reptile
was seen swimming at this Argentine locale
in 2005. [224]

LAKE DRUMSNATT MONSTER There
is a legend of a monster in this lake in
Monaghan, Ireland. A recent search of the
lake by GUST proved unsuccessful.

LAKE ESPANTOSA MONSTER A
monster described as much larger than an
alligator was supposed to have dragged a
woman into this Texas lake in 1887. [211]

LAKE GAZIVODE MONSTER In 1995
a churchgoer, walking past this artificial
Serbian lake (created 1968) saw a huge
reptilian beast. Its body was 5m long. It
had a head the size of a bull's. The witness
could not see any front legs. The back legs
looked like those of a lizard. [155]

LAKE HOPATCONG MONSTER This
was reported a couple of centuries ago in
this New Jersey lake. The head was horse
like, the body huge. It was said by
Delaware Indians to have died from falling
through ice and a boatload of settlers

claimed to have seen its carcass under the water. Yet something anomalous was espied in the lake in 1999, so there may have been more than a single monster. [S20]

LAKE MANITOU MONSTER *Add to Dictionary article* A sighting was reported in 1969 by C. Utter and her son. Reports continued up to 2006. [N/S]

LAKE MAXINKUCKEE MONSTER There was a supposed sighting of a monster in this Indiana lake in the 19th Century. [N/S]

LAKE MERRITT MONSTER This lake is a saltwater body connected to San Francisco Bay. A report of a monster in it recently, with horns and humps, about 10' in length, is being treated with a certain caution. [200]

LAKE MINNEWANKA WILDMAN A humanoid, perhaps a sasquatch, noted near this lake in Alberta towards the end of the 19th Century. It was last reported in 1899.

LAKE PEWAUKEE MONSTER A green monster reported in this Wisconsin lake in the late 19th Century. [191]

LAKE SUPERIOR MONSTER When near to Beaver Bay, on the north shore of Lake Superior, a monster with a black neck and three humps following it was seen through the trees by T. Klarenbeek. He thought it was 20'-40' long. He reported this in 2006 and likened the beast to a plesiosaur.

A photograph taken at Agawa Bay is supposed to show a couple of monsters. [N 2]

LAKE TARPON MONSTER A 10'-30' monster has been reported from this Florida lake, but descriptions vary enormously. The monster has been said to seize the odd human.

LAKE TITICACA MONSTER A creature was seen in this famous Bolivian lake in 1989. Its head was huge and its neck was 4-5m long. Its body was discerned and its tail resembled a spatula.

LAKE WAUBESA MONSTER A serpentine monster has been reported from this Wisconsin lake. [191]

LAKE WINDERMERE MONSTER In this famous English lake S. Barnip, university lecturer, and his wife saw a monster reminiscent of a serpent in August, 2006. A possible explanation is that it is a catfish, released into the water by anglers. A large pike was found on the lakeshore not long afterwards, which could possibly account for the sighting.

Sundry reports have come in of what seem to be large eels in the lake. Some are said to be larger than modern eels are supposed to be. A couple named Gaskell reported a creature that looked like a seal or dolphin without fins. Sightings of a giant creature in the lake have been occurring since 1959. Kevin Boyd, a local diver, has claimed to have seen six foot eels under water. He has also seen them in Coniston Water, which is nearby. [154 1]

LARGE OTTER-LIKE ANIMAL These carnivorous creatures have been reported from the Ozarks. [2]

LARRAKEYAH POINT SEA SERPENT Between 1946 and 1950 there was a sighting of three sea serpents at this location near Darwin, Australia. [S11]

LARSEN TRAIL CREATURE A bipedal creature of generally canine appearance encountered on two occasions between Winneconne and Oshkosh (Wisconsin). It held its upper legs or arms in front of it. [G12]

LASKOVICE Goatmen of Slavic folklore. [M]

LAVA BEAR This bear, reported from the western United States, seems to be an adaptation of the grizzly. According to a report published in 1923, a couple of specimens were killed. It has not been sighted in recent times. [A6]

LAVELLAN This was said to be an animal larger than a rat and very venomous, able to hurt cows from a distance. It is a beast of Scottish folklore. In Scottish Gaelic this creature is called *làbhallan* which can also signify a shrew, mouse or weasel. [190]

LEATHERHEAD Dog-headed creature in the folklore of Yorkshire.

LEBANON LIZARD Large unidentified lizard seen by a motorist near Lebanon

(Ohio) in 2001. [A6]

LECHUZA A witch in Texan and Mexican folklore that turns into an owl or sometimes an eagle. In one version of the legend, there was only a single Lechuza, originally a witch, who was killed. She was turned into a large bird with a human head.

LEECH LAKE MONSTER A report of a huge animal, at first mistaken for a moose, lurking in this Minnesota lake, was made in 1903. [211]

LEWIS SEA SERPENT Sea serpents have been reported from the Isle of Lewis, Scotland. One report came from a German ship in 1882. [146]

LIBAHUNT Estonian term for a werewolf.

LIFTON BIRD A large bird attacked a rider in Devon in 1990. It has been suggested it was an emu. [146]

LIGHTNING MONSTER In Zambian folklore, lightning is regarded as a monster. The front part of this beast resembles a goat, the rear part a crocodile. [R]

LIMA CENTER CANID A large unidentified animal seen in 1994 in Rock County (Wisconsin). It seemed too long for a wolf, yet wasn't a dog. It was black and hairy. It moved very quickly. [G12]

LIMA MARSH CREATURE Animal seen in Wisconsin in 2003. It was bipedal, had glowing eyes and was neither a human nor a deer. [G12]

LINCOLNSHIRE WATER BULL It would appear these creatures were once supposed to inhabit rivers in Lincolnshire. At the end of the 19th Century certain ponds in that county were referred to as bull holes. [R9]

LINDSAY LEOPARD Alleged ABC which has been reported from Lincolnshire for over ten years. All the reports, of course, may not refer to the same animal, nor is it necessarily a leopard.

LITTLEFOOT 1 In 1855 one J.W. McHenty found a tiny animal in the Maine woods. Its height did not exceed 18". The hair was long and black. He took it home

and made it a pet. Its species is a mystery.
[C27]

2 A creature that resembles bigfoot but is more gracile and the size of a child, reported from northern California. [G12]

LIZARDMAN *Add to Dictionary article*
It has been alleged that the South Carolina lizard man was merely a local in his costume, prowling about to discourage people from purloining his vegetables.

LLANGOLLEN FLYING CREATURE
A large creature resmbling a pig seen flying over Wales in 1905. The feet were webbed. [146]

LLANGORSE LAKE MONSTER There have been legends of a monster in this Welsh lake since the Middle Ages. The lake boasts some exceedingly large pike, which may lie behind the traditions. My thanks to Richard Freeman and Oll Lewis for this information.

LOBIZONI Three-legged werecow with blue eyes and a red, yellow and brown colouration said to be found near the Negro River, Brazil. [222]

LOCH BRITTLE MONSTER This was observed on the Isle of Skye in the early part of the 20th Century. It had a light on its head which have led some to speculate that it did not have a truly animal identity. [146]

LOCH GLASS MONSTER In 1730 there was supposed to be a monster in this Scottish lake.

LOCH NESS MONSTER *Add to Dictionary article* There were four alleged sightings in 2005: two in August, one in September, one in October. The last was by R. Girvan, the owner of the Loch Ness Caravan Park, who took five pictures. Mr Girvan had not previously believed in the beast. He described the head and neck as 4' tall and the colour as dark green and silvery.

   N. Clark has suggested in 2006 that early photographs allegedly of the monster were those of elephants swimming in the lake.

   The Loch Ness Monster would qualify as a protected species under the Wildlife and Countryside Act (1981). [1]

LO-LOL Monster in Abenaki Indian

legend.

LONG ISLAND CREATURE Strange
creature sighted in 2003. It was blackish
with white stripes, while the limbs were
reminiscent of a snow-leopard's. It was
about 3' tall. The witness had never seen a
lemur with its colouration and was very
doubtful that it was one. [2]

LOS CIPRESSES CREATURE A cave
at this Chilean locale was suspected to be
tenanted by a strange shapeless creature
that had exsanguinated geese. [224]

LOUGH NA CORRA CREATURES
Four of these mysterious animals, larger
than horses, were seen in the water and by
the shore of this Irish lough in 1911. [146]

LOUISIANA SATYR A woman related to
Todd Partain how she had seen a small
creature, black in colour, which reminded
her of a hairy devil. It called her name and
said it would follow her forever. This
happened near Plain Dealing. Partain was
told by another woman how her brother
caught sight of a hairy little man with
horns. His attempts to shoot it proved
futile. This young man too heard the

creature call his name. This happened at Shreveport. A correspondent of the Cryptomundo website says he saw a satyr-like being in Louisiana when he was sixteen. It looked as though its legs had elbows rather than knees, like many quadrupeds. (The only quadruped having four knees is the elephant). Its head was human-like. [200]

LUMINOUS HUMANOID There was a number of reports of such a figure or figures in Spain in 2000. [224]

LWAN In Chinese lore, a large bird of the pheasant kind, able to change its colour. [R]

LYDFORD CREATURE An animal seen on a British farm. It looked like a Great dane, had a piglike snout and slits instead of eyes. This occurred in 1983. [146]

LYTTLETON SEA MONSTER This creature, resembling an hippopotamus, was seen off the New Zealand coast in 1971. [B9]

MACON CREATURE A creature seen at night near Macon (Georgia) in 2002. It was about 3' tall and appeared to have horns, not only on its head, but on its hands. [224]

MADISON ANIMAL Two extremely large canids with heads that seemed disproportionately large and feet that appeared disproportionately small. The bodies were long and muscular. Each animal appeared to have a snout-like protruberance, which ended in a square nose. Although these creatures generally resembled dogs, their heads did not seem particularly canine. The sighting took place in 1993 or 1994 in Madison (Wisconsin). L. Godfrey notes the resemblance of these creatures to the extinct dire wolf (*Canis dirus*). [G12]

MAGAN In the traditions of Myanmar (formerly Burma) this is a sea-beast that looks like a crocodile. However, it has a pliable snout, with which it can grab you.

MAINE MUTANT *see* **Turner Beast.**

MAINE PREDATOR An unidentified creature which went on a dog-slaying career, beginning in Wales (Maine) in 2004. An animal control officer saw it and said it resembled an hyena. Puma, bobcat and lynx identities have been proposed for the animal. [200]

MALA-GILAGE Mystery tailed primates of Chad.

MALAYSIAN CREATURE A strange creature which could not be identified which was washed up on the shore of Kampung Pengalu Sungan Udang in Telok Gung on 24th January, 2006. [1]

MALIBU BEACH HUMANOID Giving an interview in 1991, the actress Shelley Winters (1920-2006) averred that, during the Second World War, a red humanoid (which at first she mistook for a frogman) stepped out of the water at this California locale and embraced her. [S11]

MAMH One of a kind of bear said to be found in Baluchistan, Pakistan. All mamhs are female. They capture male humans and force them to mate with them, the result of these unions being more mamhs. To prevent their male captives' escape, they break one of their feet. [K10]

MANBAT 1 Winged creature sighted in Wisconsin in 2006. It was sighted by a father and son driving a car along Briggs Road, Holden. Its wingspan was 10'-12' and it flew at their windscreen. It had arms and legs with claws at the end of them. Its teeth looked sharp. It let out an awful howl. Linda Godfrey has been investigating the story.

2 A creature with a canine head, seen in Texas in 2006.

MANCHE MONSTER This creature, supposedly mammalian, was harpooned in the English Channel in 1950. [155]

MANDURAH CREATURE A humanoid that was described as glistening entered a house at this locale in Western Australia in 1930. [B9]

MAN-FACED EAGLE A creature reported in Malaysia about 2002. There was one witness, a plantation recorder named Zanal. The face seemed to be the same colour of the bird's plumage. It appears to be known in local folklore. [1]

MANTINDANE A diminutive red-haired creature in the beliefs of the natives of Kenya. It drinks the blood of cattle. [C28]

MANWOLF Author Linda Godfrey, who penned the book *Beast of Bray Road* (2003), has used this word to designate the hypothetical species to which this animal may belong. She suspects it is not a werewolf, but an unknown species of bipedal canid. She has assembled a body of reports indicating the species is quite widely distributed.

One notion is that they might be the spirits of the Cheyenne Dog Soldiers, the crack troops of the Cheyenne in their defence against the encroachments of the white men.

MANY-EYED COCKATRICE This creature seems to have been no true cockatrice, as it did not project a deadly glance. However, it was covered all over with eyes. It was to be found in the region of Castle Cowys in Wales. [F5]

MANY-EYED SERPENT This was supposed to have lived in a hole at Wistonbank near Haverfordwest, Wales. [T3]

MARCOS WILD BOY A strange wild boy captured in the vicinity of Marcos in the Philippines, according to a newspaper report of 1875. The question has been posed whether he was in fact an adult specimen of *Homo floresiensis.* [200]

MARGAM CREATURE An animal seen in Wales in 2005. It was white. bigger than an Alsatian/German shepherd and its front legs were longer than its back ones. [146]

MARIA ELENA CREATURE A bizarre creature seen at this Chilean location in the early morning. It was very hairy with a number of protruding fangs. The ears were long and pointed. It had whiskers compared with those of a pig. [224]

MARIETTA BEAST An animal showing characteristics of both bear and deer seen in 2003 near Marietta (Ohio). Its legs were thin. Its snout was long. [#1]

MARLBOROUGH MONSTER New Hampshire term for a BHM.

MARSH PEOPLE The Great Marsh of Cape Cod (Massachussetss) is said to be home to creatures known as the Marsh People. Just what they are is uncertain, as is their very existence. While they may be animals, it is also possible they are primitive humans, untouched by civilization. [210]

MARSHALL GOATMAN A creature reported in the vicinity of Marshall (Texas) by hunters in 1972.

MARTIN'S BAY BIRD A mysterious blue bird seen in thus remote area of New Zealand by Alice McKenzie in 1880. It is still not known what exactly it was. One suggestion is it was the last moa. [200]

MARYLAND REPTILE Bus driver Lynda Walker saw the head of a mysterious reptilian creature in a cornfield when driving her bus along the Allibone Road in 1989. [224]

MASHERNOMAK A huge lake monster, eventually killed, in the mythology of the Menominee Indians. [R]

MASHIRAMU A large hairy being with reversed feet. It has been suggested that this trait is reported in hominids because they walk on their knuckles. It is revered as a spirit by the Yupa Indians of Colombia and Peru. [212]

MASSARUO A kind of wildman who plays the subiotto, a musical instrument, in the folklore of Cadore, Italy. [155]

MASTODON *Add to Dictionary article*
The report of a small elephant on the loose in the northern part of New York state in 1960 cannot really be held as evidence for the continued existence of the mastodon, though at least one enthusiast has advocated such an idea. However, the Stickeen Indians of Alaska assert that animals which conform to the description of the mastodon still exist.

MATAPERRO A grey animal 20' tall with a humped back bearing some resmblance to a dog. It killed livestock in Colombia in 2001.[N]

MATUHI *see* **Bush Wren.**

MAUCKS POND WHALE This unlikely cetacean was reported in a lake near East Mount Carmel (Indiana) in 1889. [N/S]

MAUSTON BIRDMAN Its body was humanoid, it had arms and legs, though its feet were like those of a bird, it had yellow feathers and a long beak. It was about 6' tall. It was seen in Wisconsin in 1980. [G12]

MAWAS *Add to Dictionary article:* The mawas is said to be 10' high, which would make it much taller than the normal orang-utan, though the possibility of giant orang-utans cannot be ruled out. (See *Cryptosup*). Mention of the mawas is to be found in the annals of the village of Kampung Mawai (Johor), which was actually named after the beast. Much excitement has been generated by the supposed sighting of a trio of mawas, including what appears to be a young one, in Johor in late 2005. A possible footprint was discovered in the Bukit Lantang woods. V. Chow, an expert in biodiversity, thinks the trio is following a path cleared by an elephant. Fur is also said to have been discovered. The state of Johor is to organise an official search. The creature is said to be non-aggressive and partially carnivorous. It is also claimed to be cleanly: it will wash off the blood of animals it has killed in rivers.

The Johor Wildlife Society claims that one of their members has observed mawas close to and made the strange observation that 70% of them resemble humans and 30% apes.. One piece of folklore says the mawas has an upside down nose. One source claims there is a colony in Johor whose progenitors moved thither from Perak because of human activity. This group was initially seventeen strong, but now numbers about forty. A large footprint has been found by J. Gates. It measured 60cm by 36cm.

A local tribe called the Orang Asli believes in them. The first actually reported sighting of a mawas was in 1871. The 2005 sightings were initially made by members of this tribe.

The idea has been put forward that mawas are actually orang-utans which have escaped from captivity. Unfortunately, purported photographs of the animal proved to be fakes. [200 1]

MERMAID *Add to Dictionary article* In 1990 two birdwatchers vanished from the island of Eynhallow in the Orkneys. It was thought by some they had been taken by mermaids. [146]

The *Shipping Gazette* in 1857 reported that a sailor had spotted a good-looking mermaid. It was believed that certain caves on the coast of Aberdeenshire were home to mermaids and a fisherman claimed to have spoken to one there in the 1870s.

A mermaid was reported regularly off Deerness in the Orkney Islands in the 1890s. The body was white, but the head black. Its length was estimated at 6'-7'. A strange mermaid, apparently wearing a shawl, was seen three times off the island of Hoy in 1913.

In Scandinavian lore, the lower part of a mermaid could be that of a porpoise rather than a fish. Scandinavians preserved the odd tradition that their male counterparts, mermen, were partial to presents, especially mittens. *See also* **Finman, Freshwater Mermaid, Mud Mermaid.**

MEXICAN BIRDMAN Two creatures that seemed to be a mixture of man and bird were seen by a woman in Nuevo Leon in 1994. The head of each creature was human. [224]

MEXICAN CREATURE A greyish-greenish creature about 4' tall with wings. Its fangs were particularly intimidating. It was seen in 1995. [154]

MICHI-PICHOUX A huge creature, apparently feline, with a beaver-like tail, said to dwell in the St Lawrence River in Cree belief. One wonders if it preserves a memory of *Castor ohioensis*, the giant beaver known to have once existed in North America. [M]

MIDGARD SERPENT The huge serpent of Norse myth which was the son of the trickster god Loki. Odin threw him into the ocean and the Norsemen believed he encircled the world.

MIGAS Tentacled and dangerous river monster, reported to live in the Congo. [M]

MILCHAM In Jewish legend, a bird based on the Phoenix. It is consumed by flames, leaving an egg from which the next Milcham grows, just as in the Phoenix legend. In the Jewish tale, it was the only creature that didn't eat from the Tree of Life.

MILLERSPORT CAT Mystery animal reported from central Ohio from 2001. The colour was given as grey and black. It has been suggested that the animal was, not a cat, but a coyote. [2]

MINAS GERAIS HUMANOID This apparently transparent humanoid, seen in Passo Tempo, Brazil, in 1950, was apparently able to run unscathed through a barbed-wire fence. It fled into a wood. [224]

MINERVA MONSTER A BHM reported in Stark County (Ohio) from 1978.

MINOTAUR *Add to Dictionary article*
At some stage the Cretans seem to have adopted the belief that the Minotaur was a doughty man named Taurus (Greek *tauros*=bull). The Etruscans seem to have harboured a tradition that the creature was killed by Hercules rather than Theseus. Minos and the Minotaur may in origin be the same character, the latter the king conceived in bull form. It is not impossible the bull cult was ultimately brought to Greece from Catal Huyuk, the early city in Anatolia, where a bull cultus seems to have been practised. The Luwata Berbers worshipped a bull-headed god called Agurzil.

MIQQJAYUUQ A hairy, lake-dwelling creature in Eskimo belief. They say it lacks a face. [M]

MIRKA Alternative name for the yeti.

MISSOURI PTEROSAUR A possible creature spotted from Farmington (Mo.). The witness, a child at the time, seems sensible, admitting the possibility of error. [2]

MITCHELL RIVER MONSTER A tall creature, perhaps a hominid, reported from near Mitchell River (North Carolina). [200]

MIZORAM CREATURE Mystery animals resembling rats, described as weird, have been on the loose in the village of Aizaol in Mizoram, India. [1]

MOCKING LAKE MONSTER A monster has been reported in this Quebecois lake. It is said to have a saw-tooth fin on its back. It is known to locals. [2]

MOHA MOHA *Add to Dictionary article* In fact, the original name given to the animal by Miss Lovell was *moka-moka*, which is a plausible Aborigine name.

MOHAWK MYSTERY ANIMAL A creature that wrecked a car in New York state in 2007. It may have been pursuing cats. [200]

MOHOAO Alternative term for a maero.

MOKELE-MBEMBE *Add to Dictionary article* It has been said that the creature prefers to stay under water. It may have an occipital frill. It has now been argued that we are perhaps dealing here with a mammal rather than a reptile.

MOKELUMNE RIVER MONSTER A monster in this river in Nevada was said to have killed a Chinese fisherman in the 19th Century. [A6]

MOLUNKUS MONSTER According to a report made in 1887, a creature seen in the vicinity of South Molunkus (Maine). It was 6'-7' long, with a lengthy neck and tail and a brownish colour. It left tracks which resembled those of a wolf, but which were larger. [200]

MOMPIES A river monster supposedly found in the Sterkspruit, a river in the Free State Province, South Africa. It is reptilian, has a blue-green head and is covered with slime. Its back bears a hump. Its tail resembles that of a lizard. [193]

MONKEY BEAR Nebraska term for a BHM.

MONKEY-EATING TREE Carnivorous tree of Brazil said to devour monkeys and other animals.

MONKEY-FACED BIRD A giant bird whose face resembled a monkey's, reported in Oregon. [BB]

MONSTER TROUT In Ainu belief, a large fish capable of swallowing a deer or a bear. The gods brought it ashore, where humans killed it. [B21]

MONSTER TURTLE A large beast rumoured to lurk in Lester Milligan Park, Mason City (Iowa). [1]

MONTANA VARMINT This creature, reported in 1892, seems to have had some humanoid characteristics and was at least partially bipedal. It was said to eat bears and mountain sheep. [200]

MONTAUK POINT SEA SEPENT A sea monster seen off Long Island (NY) in 1929. [B9]

MONTECRISTO CREATURE
Montecristo is near Tocopilla in Chile.
Here in June 2001 a monster 2m tall with
an animal head and huge wings flew
alongside a driving family. At times the
speed was 100km per hour. [224]

MONTENEGRIN WILDMAN In 1996
S. Spasovic and D. Radulav claim to have
seen a wildman on the Frusta Gorn
mountain in Montenegro. It was hairy and
nearly 3m tall. Folklorist V. Ognjenoviae
claimed to have met a countryman many
years ago who claimed to have seen a
wildman in the same country. [155]

MOOGIE Reptilian monster said to live in
the Ozarks. [R]

MOON MAN Term for a BHM used in
Warren and Dekalb Counties (Tennessee).

MOOSE-COW HYBRID A creature born
in 1939 was suspected of being a cross
between a moose and a cow, but it was
probably merely a cow. [#12]

MOOSE-HORSE HYBRID Although
such a hybrid is regarded as genetically
impossible, in 2006 a strange creature was

born to a mare in Quebec. The only stallions on the farm concerned had been neutered. The animal's head and legs were moose-like. Mooses and horses will mate, but such matings should not prove fruitful. The animal has been called Bambi. [2]

MOSQUITO-MAN In the legends of South America, a creature which sucks blood from animals through its nose. [190]

MOTHMAN *Add* A Mothman museum which is the recipient of Mothman reports has opened in Point Pleasant.

MOUND CITY BIRD A bird allegedly killed near Mound City (Kentucky) in 1868. Its head was bright redd, its down white, its wings black and its beak yellow. It was said to be larger than an ostrich, yet it was apparently capable of flight, for it had been perched on a tree branch. [1]

MOUNT ADAMS BIRD An unidentified brown bird, 7' tall, reported from Washington state in 1975. [N]

MOUNT BEST HUMANOID Black creature, somewhat human in shape with bright, white eyes, seen twice (by the same witness) near Mount Best, Australia, in 2006. [223]

MOUNTAIN MAN A BHM of Japanese tradition. [R]

MOXIE MOUNTAIN CREATURE A small humanoid, 3' to 4' tall, seen on this mountain in Maine some years ago. [#9]

MUC-SHEILC Monster said to be found in Loch Maree, Scotland. Others of this species are said to be found in other lochs.

MULE SEM CABESA In Brazilian folklore, a woman who transforms into a headless mule on Thursday nights. This is as a punishment for some wickedness.

MULJEWANG Lake and river monster of Australian Aboriginal lore. Look out for it if you happen to be sailing along the Murray. [M]

MULLICA RIVER CREATURE As canoists were canoing (as canoists do) one day in Mullica River (NJ), they were followed on shore by a mystery creature that kept under cover. [M12]

MULLUMBIMBY CREATURE At this Australian locale, this animal was observed by motorist Barbara Eady in 2005. At first she thought it was a dog, then revised her opinion. She said the head was strange and the animal odd-looking. Its back sloped. She was sure it wasn't a dog or a fox. [206]

MUD MERMAID Two creatures so called were reported from the banks of the Ohio in 1891. They appeared to be a male and a female. The male's body was described as being much like a human's. Its back tapered behind the legs, but did not become a tail. Its arms were shorter than its legs. There was hair on its back. Its face was like a human's, but its eyes lacked the sparkle human consciousness imparts. [N/S]

MUMUGA A creature of Australian Aboriginal lore. Its arms and legs are short, causing it problems with speedy locomotion, but it could fart continuously, causing the Aborigine it planned to devour to be overcome. [X]

MUNGKORN Thai name for a dragon.

MUNGOON-GALLI Mysterious lizard,

said to be a monitor, reported from New South Wales.

MUSTELINE CREATURE A grey creature with a musteline face and about the size of a squirrel with a stubby tail was seen in Pennsylvania. The report (not the incident) was dated 2004. [2]

MYROSS BAY CREATURE This irish animal looked like a cat with a hairless tail. It was the size of a dog. It was blamed for killing chickens in 1921. [146]

MYSTERY FISH The website *Cryptomundo* has displayed a photograph of this animal, allegedly caught in the south-eastern USA. The photograph was on a postcard apparently datable to the period between 1904 and 1918. The identity of the creature has produced various suggestions and it may not even be a fish at all, as it bears some resemblance to, though is the wrong colour for, the aquatic animal variously known as the elephant's trunk snake, wart snake or file snake (*Acrochordus javanicus*) which is found in Asia.

MYSTERY FOX A strange pink-looking

fox of which a photograph of unknown provenance has been circulated. It may be a grey fox (*Urocyon*) which has lost its hair or is short-haired. [2]

MYSTERY UTAH CREATURE In March 2005 this unidentified creature crossed the road in front of astonished motorist D. Hansen, who said it was tall and dark with long hair. This occurred at Diamond Mountain Flats. [189]

MYSTIC RIVER CREATURE A creature 3'-4' long with bulging eyes which frightened rwo teenage girls. [154]

NARGUN Go carefully if you are in the vicinity of the Mitchell River in Australia. In a cave behind a waterfall lives, so the Guner Aborigines will tell you, the Nargun. It is large, it is female and aboriginal weapons are useless against it. [190]

NARRABEEN CRITTER In 1968 this was observed by a witness at Narrabeen Lakes, a suburb of Sydney, Australia. It was standing in the shallows of a lake. Its skin and back legs were like an elephant's and it had short forelegs. It then quitted the lake. [S11]

NAUI Bird of Russian legend, perhaps a mixture of eagle and dragon. [D4]

N-DAM-KENO-WET A half-human, half-fish creature with long hair in the legends of the Abenaki Indians.

NEE-GUED Name for a humanoid, perhaps a yeti, in Sikkim, a once independent country which was taken over by India. [M]

NET-NET Small clawed humanoids in the beliefs of the Australian Aborigines of Victoria. [X]

NEW BRUNSWICK WATER ANIMAL A strange two-legged creature, perhaps a primate, seen under water in 1973. It appeared to be covered in black fur. Its skin is described as crusty. [230]

NEW CALEDONIAN BOOBOOK A bird which is known only from bones, but which may not yet be extinct, despite a lack of reports of living specimens.

NEW JERSEY GARGOYLE A quadrupedal hominid seen in New Jersey

was definitely identified as a gargoyle by a
Maine newspaper in 1909. It is doubtless
the case that the writer was well versed in
the physiology of gargoyles. [A7]

NEWBERG CREATURE Seen in
Newberg (Oregon) in 2005, this humanoid
was not tall and looked as if its skin had
been burned. It jumped over the bonnet of
a car and departed. [224]

NEWHAVEN BHM *See* Sussex
Wildman.

NGOLIBA HOMINID These hominids
have been reported from eleven forests in
Kenya. [B9]

NGOUBOU An animal about the size of
an ox, allegedly found in Cameroon. They
live in herds and fight elephants. They
have horns on their faces, but the
inhabitants maintain they are distinct from
the rhinoceros. [190]

NICKUR A dangerous water creature of a
supernatural character in Icelandic
tradition. Its hooves are back to front.
Mount it and it will jump into the sea with
you. [C12]

NIGER DINOSAUR A small creature, thought to be a young, killed at Arlit, Niger, at an unspecified date. It had spines on its back and a thick, strong tail. [154]

NIGHT PARROT An Australian bird (*Pezoporus occidentalis*) which may or may not be extinct. A dead specimen was reported in 2006.

NINE-HEADED DRAGON Polycephalous creature of Lithuanian legend.

NINGYO In Japanese belief, a kind of merbeing with a human head, the rest of its body being piscine. [213]

NINKI-NANKA *Add to Dictionary article* There is some possibility that this term is used for different animals in different places. One description gives it a horse's face, a long neck and tail and a reptilian body. Sometimes it is conceived as a snake. Some say it has a horn, some that its head sports a diamond. Crests have also been said to cover the creature's head. They seem to frequent swamps and there seems to be some sort of idea that they live in holes. Some say it has not merely one horn, but three. The recent J.T. Downes Memorial Expedition (2006) came to the conclusion that the ninki-nanka was extinct in the lower Gambia. However, it decided it was possibly still to be found in more southerly regions, such as Guinea. A truck accident said to have occurred in 2001 or later is supposed to have been caused by the ninki-nanka's crossing the road in front of the vehicle. [#9 1]

NISSEQUOGUE CREATURE A strange white creature spotted at night by C. Meister and another witness (unnamed) on Long Island (NY). It was bipedal, had pointed ears and a long tail. Mr Meister noted some resemblance between the animal and a kangaroo. [154]

NJAGO GUNDA Water monster of African tradition, said to be twice the size of an elephant. It appears to have some sort of trunk, from which it fires a fierce jet of water. [A6]

NORMANGEE GOATMAN A 7' tall humanoid with the horns and hooves goat, but otherwise looking human with light hair all over was seen in 2002 from a window in

Texas. [154]

NORTH ALBERTA CREATURE
Animal seen in Canada by a horsewoman in
1998. She identified it as an hyena, but not
all commentators were sure she was correct.
[2]

NOXIE MONSTER Oklahoma name for
a BHM.

NUE In Japanese mythology, a creature
combining features of monkey, tanuki, tiger
and snake. It can fly, but has to turn into a
black cloud to do so.

NUKUPU'U A bird (*Hemignathus
lucidus*) of Hawaii, now probably, but not
certainly, extinct.

NURE-ONNA Dangerous sea-monster of
Japanese lore.

NYOKODOING A felid, perhaps a water-
dwelling sabretooth, reported from Sudan.

NZE TI GOU A mysterious water creature
said to be found in the Congo (Kinshasa).

OACHITA GIANT WOLF Such

creatures have been reported from the Ozarks. [2]

OAHU PTEROSAUR A pterodactyl-like creature seen by soldiers in the Kahuku Range of Oahu (Hawaii). The sighting probably took place in 1999. [2]

OAKHAM CAT An ABC, white with tan patches, seen in Rutland in 2001. [H18]

OCTIPOS The name given by C. Rafinesque (1783-1840) to a strange creature seen in the Atlantic in 1818. Its head was 2' in length and its body a further 56'. It had eight gills. Its head and neck stuck out of the water. Rafinesque thought another creature, also seen in the Atlantic, might be a type of octipos.

OCTOFOLK Merbeings, the upper half resembling a human, the lower half an octopus's tentacles. The female is called an *octomaid*, the male an *octoman*. [213]

ODENTON HUMANOID Creature of brown/black colouration encountered at Odenton (Maryland) in 1989. It was about 4' tall and had a white stripe on its leg. [224]

OHIO RIVER ANIMAL Unusual aquatic cryptid spotted by two boys in the Ohio River in Henderson County (Kentucky) in the 1980s. It had a head with a protruding snout and black eyes followed by several humps sticking out of the water. It seems to have been of a green colour and it undulated horizontally. The creature has been seen on a number of occasions, one of the witnesses being cryptozoologist B.M. Nunelly. There seems to be more than one specimen concerned. [A6]

OLD MILL POND MONSTER This body of water is near Trenton (NJ). A monster is said to have been sighted here in 1975. [N]

OLD SLIPPERYSKIN A creature resembling a bear of immense size in Vermont folklore. [A7]

OLOMAO A bird (*Myadestes lanaiensis*) from Hawaii, which is now probably, but not certainly, extinct. [Audubon WatchList]

OMAHA CREATURE An unidentified animal photographed by Mary Ann Carth in her garden in Omaha (Nebraska) in June, 2006. [2]

ONCA A mystery cat of Brazil, said to favour the jungle depths. It is rarely seen and quite distinct from a jaguar or puma. Its coat, which is partially spotted, is of a light colouration. [200]

ONE-EYED APE A cyclopean pithecoid creature with a prehensile tail reported in Jessamine County (Kentucky). The animal was seen by a single witness in 1831. [209]

ONE-EYED DRAGON Its eye was very large and it lived at Casrle Carlton in Wales. [F5]

ONE-HORNED BULL A large animal in the legends of the Evenks of Russia.

ONE-HORNED CREATURE The writer Ibn Fadlan (10th Century) describes an animal which he claimed existed in his day in Russia. It had the body of a mule, a ram's head, a single horn and a bull's tail. Although hostile to humans, its diet was vegetarian. It has been suggested that the creature represents a surviving population of the elasmotherium, a prehistoric animal resembling a rhinoceros, but scientists would treat such an assertion with caution.

ONGUIRIRA An animal seen in the 1850s in present day Namibia. Its resemblance to a puma was noticed. Natives said it did not attack humans. A similar creature, not given this name, was mentioned by F. Galton *Narrative of an Explorer in Tropical South Africa* (1853). [2]

ORANGE BIG CAT This was seen in Borders, Scotland, in 2006. It was larger than an adult fox. [F12]

OROBON According to travel lore, this was a cat-headed creature with a crocodile's body to be found in Arabia. [M]

ORPHIR SEA CREATURE Beast seen off the Orkney Islands in the 1850s. Its head was flat, its teeth menacing. It was adorned with a mane. The witness was a boy called Alec Groundwater. The creature tried to seize him by the legs. [208]

OSTERHASE The Easter Hare in German folklore. From this the Easter Bunny evolved.

'O'U An Hawaiian bird which is possibly but not certainly extinct, as it has not been reported since the 1980s.

OWENIKEN LAKE MONSTER Monster reported from this British Columbia lake. Clayton Mack, a respected citizen of Bella Coola, was the source of information about it. [2]

OYSTER BAY CLOUD Although it looked like a cloud, this creature was apparently alive and shot water at the witness. It was seen at Oyster Bay, Long Island, in 1975.

PAIYUK Water dwelling wapiti of huge size in the legends of the Ute Indians. Paiyuks are dangerous to man. [M]

PANLONG Water dragons, generally to be found in lakes, in Chinese belief.

PAPUAN DRAGON Creature as tall as a double-decker bus, the object of belief in Papua-New Guinea. [1]

PARAINEN ISLAND MONSTER A creature seen off this Finnish island in

1979. [B9]

PAVARÓ A dog-headed creature or spirit in the folklore of the north of Italy. [A6]

PAYNE COUNTY CREATURE This looked rather like an ostrich. Its head resemble, but wasn't identical with, a horse's. It was seen near Ripley (Oklahoma) in 1999. [230]

PECOS PUEBLO SNAKE According to J. Abert, writing in 1846, this giant reptile was kept by the Indians here and fed babies. J. Gregg claimed to have seen its tracks in the snow. [200]

PENARTH CREATURE A woman from Penarth, Wales, was scared by a large creature spread out like a bird on the wall of her garden. The witness claimed the creature was several metres long. [1]

PENDLETON ANIMAL A strange animal, fur-bearing and quadrupedal, shot in Oregon in October 2000. The skeleton was analysed by the US Fish and Wildlife Service, but the result was not released. [1]

P'ENG-NIAO Creature of Chinese belief,

combining elements of bird and dragon. [219]

PENISTONE CAT An ABC coloured white with a beige tail seen in Yorkshire in 1999. [H18]

PESANTA Huge dog or cat in Catalan folklore, which will lie on a person's chest, giving him nightmares. This creature may have been invented to explain the condition of sleep paralysis, which is not uncommon. [190]

PETTICOAT LOOSE A horse with a woman's head, bearing this singular name, is said to dwell in a pond amidst the Knockmealdown Mountains in Ireland. [146]

PEUCHEN In Mapuche Indian mythology, this was sometimes regarded as a giant flying snake. It seemed to have the power to change into other creatures. A medicine man drove it away. [190]

PEVENSEY MARSHES ANIMALS Before the Second World war, grey creatures, which some said were the hybrids of wolves and foxes, were reported in this

area. Some said they were werewolves.
[146]

PHANTOM KANGAROO *Add to Dictionary article* Although out of place kangaroos are rarely caught, an exception occurred in Iowa in 2005. The kangaroo was placed in the Vila Real Zoo.

A 1974 encounter between a mystery kangaroo and police officers in Chicago was the first of several sightings in Illinois and Wisconsin. In Canada, such kangaroos were seen in 1968 and 1979. One was reported in Yorkshire in 1989. In 2006 an out-of-place kangaroo was reported in England in the *Cornish Times.* However, it may have been a wallaby. A recent report of a phantom kangaroo has come in from Austria, while one was seen in Hungary in 1985.

PHUKU-PHUKA Apparently a bird of some kind which, in a Bechuana tale, saved children from an ogre. [W2]

PI' CANG CO'I A hairy wildman, usually about 5' tall, nocturnal in habit, reported from Vietnam. [1]

PIASA *Add to Dictionary article* Others

are also said to have found Russell's bone-strewn cave, but it has now disappeared, perhaps submerged by encroaching forest. Other sightings of the pictographs were reported by St Cosmo (1686) and Stoddard (1812). A huge bird - a lingering piasa? - was espied over Alton in 1948. There was another sighting of a large avian in 2003. [T4]

PIATEK In Armenian legend, a large animal of the days of yore. It had a beak, but was nonetheless mammalian. [190]

PIHUECHENYI Winged snakes with vampiric tendencies in Araucanian legend. [M]

PITTSBURGH CREATURE An unidentified animal reported in Pittsburgh (Pa). Its face was described as resembling that of either a bear or a weasel. It was stubtailed, grey and hairy. [2]

PLAGUE ANIMAL In the Middle Ages, although it was known the Black Death was transmitted, no one knew how this happened. One theory was that an animal, its nature unguessed, would run through the village, leaving the plague in its wake.

PLUM CREEK CREATURE A mystery animal of Louisiana legend. No description is to hand.

POINT PLEASANT BIRD Gigantic unidentified bird reported from West Virginia in 1967. [N]

POMPTON LAKES CREATURE This was seen along Route 287 in New Jersey. Its face resembled that of an armadillo and it proceeded by hopping. This occurred in 1995. [M12]

PORT STEPHENS SEA SERPENT A yellow coloured sea monster which proceeded in loops was seen here, off the Australian coast, in 1925 by those aboard a ship. The sighting was quite lengthy, lasting a quarter of an hour. [B9]

POTOMAC HIGHLANDS MYSTERY CREATURE An unidentified animal photographed on August 8th, 2006, in West Virginia. It may have been a puma. The photograph is reproduced on the website *Cryptomundo*. [200]

PRAIRIE DEVIL Small mystery lizard

alleged to have been seen at the Fountain River at Pueblo (Colorado). Photographic evidence was supplied, but the sender, who corresponded entirely be e-mail, disappeared. Local tradition is not altogether silent about such an animal, but is scarce. [A6] Do not confuse with the beast so called in *Dictionary.*

PUERTO RICO GOATMAN According to the website *Crop Circle Research*, a goatman has been reported in Puerto Rico.

PUGOT Headless giant of Filipino lore. As explained elsewhere, a creature may appear headless if it holds its head below the level of its shoulders. It is often said to be seen carrying the heads of others.

PYBUS BAY DWARF A small hairy humanoid in which the Tlingit Indians of Admiralty Islands believe. [X]

PYRASSOUPI A creature reported from Arabia in the 16th Century. It is, however, a kind of paradox, as it is described as a unicorn with two horns. Its fur was said to resemble that of a bear, but otherwise it looked like a mule. [R]

QAXDASCIDI This beast, of which there seems to be no description, lurks beneath the frozen waters of Alaska and makes notable noises, according to the Indians. [R]

QUAKER CAT A cat larger than a domestic, which makes an awful screaming noise. It is said to be found in Massachussetts. [2]

QUAZER BEAST The Enets of Siberia say that this monster was a serpent that dwelt in the Arctic Ocean. Two horns stuck out from the back of its head. If anyone tried to enter the mouth of the Yenisei River, the Quazer Beast formed a powerful obstacle. [190]

QUEENS COUNTY CREATURE A New Brunswick creature that attacked one Herman Balyea in 1951. It was black or grey and its tail was estimated at 2'. It stood on its hind legs to attack, but was driven off by Balyea. [224]

QUEENSTOWN PREDATOR A mystery animal that in 1971 killed both a Shetland pony and a large pig in Alabama. [B9]

QUILLOTA CREATURE Creature 90cm in height, looking like a noseless centaur, reported from Chile in 2000. [224]

RABUN COUNTY CREATURE A hominid with bluish hair and large ears, but apparently deaf, was reported from this area in Georgia (USA). [A7]

RAM-HORNED BEAST A bipedal creature with a face like a sheep's and ram-like horns. It was seen in West Virginia in the 1990s. [#1]

RASKOVIC In the realm of cryptobotany, this is a kind of grass in the folklore of the Serbs. It has the power to open locks. [190]

RATMAN This creature is said to lurk in the Mills Reservation (New Jersey). It is said to have a human head and the four-legged body of a large man. Once, it is said, it was a normal man. It is only seen for a couple of months each year. One suggests it lives in the sewers. It gives tongue to horrible ululations. [S20]

RATTLE-SNAKE BUSH Said to be

found in Mexico, this bush is alleged to encircle its victims, human and animal, in its coils and sting them to death. [225]

RAVENNA MONSTER A monster reported from the vicinity of this Italian city. It had a human head and torso and had a single scaly leg (or else a pair of legs of which one only was scaly) with an extra eye in it. It had wings instead of arms. [R]

RAYAS Humanoid race with their mouths in their navels, said to be found in South America near the River Sinapo, a tributary of the Orinoco. [Z]

RAYSTOWN LAKE MONSTER
Raystown Lake in Pennsylvania allegedly contains a monster, of which a photograph appeared in 2006. However, as the lake was created only in 1912, it has been suggested by some that the monster is a hoax, intended to lure tourists into the area. [200]

RECIFE SEA SERPENT A monster reported off the Brazilian coast in 1906 by a ship. It had huge dorsal fins and travelled with astonishing speed. [B9]

RED BIRD A bird the size of a (?barn) owl, which the witness could not identify, seen near Hull, England. It was a foot tall and had a small beak. It flew off after a few seconds.

RED MONKEY A creature of aggressive nature, supposedly to be found in Congleton (Devon) in times gone by. [146]

REINDEER LAKE MONSTER
Although this lake in Manitoba is no longer visited by reindeer, there is a tradition that a monster living in Deep Bay used to eat them as they fell through the ice. There have been a number of sightings. Recent killings of dogs have been connected with the monster.

RIANSEAU Guinea-Bissau name for the ninki-nanka.

RICHIBACTO SEA-SERPENT This was seen off New Brunswick in 1891. Its length was estimated at 200'. Its head was flat with froglike eyes on top. [200]

RIDGEWAY MONSTER Ridgeway is a small town in Michigan. There have been reports there of a creature with red hair and grey eyes that looks through windows, affrighting those within.

RIO GRANDE CITY CREATURE A creature seen in this Texan town in 1975. It was described as half human, half bird. [BB]

RIPLEY CREATURE A noisy creature was seen at this Oklahoma site in 1999. Its head resembled a horse's, its body an ostrich's. [224]

ROAD-CROSSING BEAST There have been two sightings of a similar animal that appears to have been canine, but was too large to be a wolf, seen in Wisconsin running in a smooth manner across the road. The first sighting was in 1991, the second in 1993 or 1994. The fur was shaggy. There seem to have been other sightings. Linda Godfrey calls this creature a road runner, but I have avoided this so there will be no confusion with the well-known bird of the same name (*Geococcyx*), as frequently to be seen in cartoon form, outwitting what must be the most luckless Coyote on the planet. [G12]

ROARING WHALE A strange cetacean,

which did not blow but roared, was reported in 1896 to have attacked a ship. It may have been as long as 80' and it had a broad head, tapering to a point, giving it a very different configuration from other, known kinds of whale. The captain opined that, in the distance, it might have been mistaken for a sea serpent. [A6]

ROCK MAN According to the Miwok Indians, this creature lived in the California Caverns and would seize and eat humans.

ROCK RIVER MONSTER This river flows in Wisconsin. The monster which occupies it features in Winnebago Indian legend. It is serpentine, some having thought there was more than one of them. The monster was said to have horns and claws. Some say they still exist, living underneath the Mississippi in habitats dug from the banks. [191 G12]

ROCKAWAY CREATURE A creature of raccoon size, but completely black, graceful of movement, spotted in Rockaway (NJ) about 2004. [2]

ROCKAWAY SHOALS SEA SERPENT A monster seen off Long Island (NY) in

1913. [B9]

ROLDAN CREATURE A small hairy humanoid seen by two women in a motor-car in Argentina in 1997. It jumped over the road. [224]

RONG Vietnamese name for a dragon.

RONGWE TIGER Mystery striped animal rumoured to be found in Tanzania. That it is an hyena or aardwolf seems unlikely, as it is outside their ranges. [#9]

ROSWALR Horse-headed whale-like creature of Norwegian folklore, ultimately based on the walrus.

ROSWELL CREATURE Although this report was made in 2006, it does not give the actual date of the incident. North-east of Roswell an unidentified reptilian creature, perhaps 3' high, was seen. [154]

ROUTE 35 MONSTER Seen in West Virginia, this was a creature that proceeded on all fours, was white and was bigger than a dog. A sighting of what may have been this animal was made in Four States, in the same state. [#1]

RUJIGAR This is said to be an alternative name for the Nandi bear (see *Dictionary*).

RUKI Kiribati name for a sea serpent.

RUSSIAN CHUPACABRAS A creature that exsanguinates its victims has been reported from Russia and obvious comparisons with the chupacabras have been made. In 2005, 32 turkeys were killed and drained of blood. The "Russian chupacabras" was observed by Yerbulet Isbasov who gave its height as 1.2m. He also said it was humped. A pack of the creatures was seen by another witness, consisting of one red and one grey specimen with a number of young. Scientists could not identify photographs of footprints. The report gives the location of these matters as "central Russia" without being more specific. [Mosnews.com]

RUSSIAN RIVER LIZARD A 7"-8" tall lizard that stood upright and looked like a tiny tyrannosaurus was seen in 1951 near the Russian River (California). [A6]

RUSSIAN WILDMAN Wildmen were observed in the village of Kolomenskoye,

Russia, in 1566. Such creatures were supposed to have entered this universe through a portal in Golosovyi gully. In 1825 it was said that two men actually slipped into a parallel world through this portal, but were helped to return by a hairy humanoid. They thought they had been gone for only a day, but found twenty years had passed since their departure. This is often a feature of folktales, where time goes at a different rate in different universes. [224]

SABINE RIVER MONSTER A strange creature photographed near the mouth of the Sabine River, which forms the border between Texas and Louisiana, in 2006. It was said to be swimming on its back and the photographer estimated its length at 45'. It had a somewhat serpentine appearance. A catfish identity seems to be ruled out. [200]

SABINE THING A grey creature resembling an ape reported from Sabine (Texas) in 2000. [154]

SACRED FISH These were supposed to be found in two wells in Wales, Mary's Well and Peter's Well. [T3]

SAIVO-NEITA Naid in Lapp/Saami belief.

SAKHALIN CREATURE A large sea monster was allegedly hauled out of the sea near Sakhalin off the Pacific coast of Russia. It was nearly 7m long and grey-skinned. The captain involved said it resembled a plesiosaur. Similarities have, however, been noted between its skull and that of a beluga. [200]

SALT LAKE CITY SNAKE A snake with small wings, coloured brown with purple stripes, with a tail split into two, was encountered by T. Miller in Salt Lake City. He felt it made telepathic contact with him, seeking help. [189]

SALVANCHO Savage hairy wildman of Italian folklore. [155]

SAN BENITO GIANT BIRD There have been various reports of this bird at this Texan locale since 1945. It is said to have black feathers, while the underside is white. The face is like that of a cat. It is aggressive towards people. [BB]

SAN DIEGO TROUGH FISH A huge creature, 30'-40' in length, which approached a submersible in the eastern Pacific. The size of its eyes was compared with that of dinner plates. [B]

SAN JUAN GARGOYLE San Juan is the capital of Puerto Rico, a place where many strange entities have been reported. A 5' humanoid, grey with wings, had a fight with a policeman when discovered consuming a rat. (It was the creature consuming the rat, not the policeman). It had wings and escaped by flying. This happened in 1995. [224]

SAN LUIS CREATURE Seen in the San Luis Valley (Colorado) in 1993, this was a hairy creature with big ears which were pointed. It had long arms. It was humanoid. [224]

SAOS Gigantic humans who once supposedly lived in Chad. Funerary jars containing gigantic human bones were allegedly found there in 1936.

SAR MAYEE Legendary ox of Myanmar, noted for the length of its hair.

168

SARANAC LAKE MONSTER At a time when this lake in New York state was apparently icebound, this animal is said to have popped its head out of a hole in the ice. [2]

SARPA Reptilian race in Indian tradition.

SCHERGER CREATURE A creature seen in Queensland, Australia, by air force personnel at night. It could not be identified. The front legs were longer than the back. It seemed to be spotted. Such cryptids as thylacoleo and thylacine have been suggested as identities, as has an out of place hyena or even a wild pig. [2]

SCOTT TOWN MONSTER This creature was reported in 2007 in Jamaica. It had a long face and a snout, four narrow legs and was said to be twice the size of a dog. The animal seems keen on consuming pumpkins and melons. Dogs fall silent when it approaches. [1]

SCREAMING KANGAROO These creatures were sometimes said to have characteristics of a dog or pterodactyl. They were reported from various western parts of the United States in the 1950s.

SEA BEASTS OF SRI LANKA The
Romans had contact with Sri Lanka, in
Latin called *Taprobane*. The naturalist
Aelian remarked that there were strange sea
creatures about its coasts, with the bodies of
fish and the heads of lions, leopards, wolves
and rams. These are probably distorted
descriptions of real creatures or perhaps
mere traveller's tales. To avoid confusion, I
will remind the reader that Sri Lanka was
formerly called *Ceylon* and *Serendib.*

SEA CATTLE In Orcadian folklore, the
cattle living in the sea, property of the
finmen.

SEA CREATURE In 1957 a team led by
E. de Bisschop was travelling by raft from
Tahiti to Chile. One day tey found an
unidentified creature on deck, standing on
its tail.   It dived back into the sea. [N]

SEA GIANT In Fiji, gigantic human
footprints leading from the sea were
discovered around the beginning of March,
2006, but whatever creature made them has
apparently not been seen. [1]

SEA HORSE An undersea dwelling horse, property of the finmen, in the lore of the Orkney Islands.

SEA SERPENT *Add to Dictionary article* Another classification system has been attempted by B. Champagne. The latter is sceptical that many of his categories represent genuine creatures.

In Indian belief, the sea serpents have a king called Dhumavarna.

SEACORN Alternative name for the sea unicorn.

SEAL-EATING KILLER WHALE An unrecorded variety of killer whale suspected to live in Antarctic waters. [#9]

SECOND MESA MONSTER On the Hopi reservation in Arizona is a cave containing a deep water hole. This is said to contain a monster that once snatched a child.

SECURITY BAY SEA SERPENT Sea serpent reported off the Alaska coast in 1947. [B9]

SEDJA This animal seems to be a form of

serpopard, a creature which features in Egyptian iconography. Its head seems more serpentine than that of the conventional serpopard. Depictions of it have turned up in Beni Hasan and Bershah.

SEDONA CREATURE A reptilian creature, behaving like a fugitive, was seen near Sedona (Arizona) in 1994. Later men in quasi-military uniforms were seen, perhaps looking for it. [224]

SEEFER A whale shaped like a coffin, said to be seen off the Shetland Islands from time to time. [1]

SEKLO-BALI Literally, "bed-carrier". Unknown flying creature of Papua-New Guinea, possibly identical with the ropen.

SEMARGL Large winged dog in Slavic mythology.

SENGBEH ANIMAL A fierce, unidentified animal killed several humans in Sierra Leone in 2005. When it was at length killed by police, they said it resembled a leopard, as though they had some doubts as to what it really was. [12]

SERBIAN WATER BULL According to legend, this creature lived in Lake Severa Bara, but would come ashore. It was killed by locals 250 years ago. [155]

SEROU Kind of unicorn allegedly found in Tibet. [R]

SERPOPARD An animal known from Egyptian predynastic iconography, though whether it is mythical or based on a real creature is uncertain. The predynastic period is generally thought to have ended about 3000 BC. It is shown with a feline body and long, serpentine neck. It is certainly not a giraffe, despite a superficial resemblance. Depictions of the creature have also been found in Iraq. [#9]

SETONTOT A mystery animal, of which no description has been furnished, which exists in the lore of the Orang Asli of Malaysia. The lack of description is due to the fact that you are unlikely to survive your encounter with it. It is said to hide in the earth and attack passers-by. Somehow the notion has grown up that it is 2m long.[200 201]

SEVIENDRA A bird somewhat like the

phoenix and, like that bird, consumed by fire, then regenerated. It had holes in its beak. It was said to live in India. [R]

SHEEP-SQUATCH A strange creature reported from West Virginia. Witness Ed Rollins saw it, partially hidden by trees. It was moving on four legs and had a brace of long, pointed horns. Its forefeet were like hands. He could not see the rear of the animal due to foliage. The animal had paused to take a drink. Another witness claimed to have seen a similar beast attacking a car. [#1]

SHELLICAN A creature said to inhabit West's Lake on Nelson Island in British Columbia. Long known in Indian folklore, it was apparently seen twice by one John West. He said the head was calf-sized and the face reminded him of a monkey, The cheeks were yellow. About 6' of the back was visible. [A6]

SHENANGO VALLEY CREATURE Its eyes reminded people of fish, it was well endowed with teeth, the hair was black and patchy and the elbow and knee joints were like a dog's. It was sometimes bipedal and had no tail. It was reported in Pennsylvania from 1972-1998. [G12]

SHISAA A kind of doglike animal with leonine aspects in the mythology of the island of Okinawa. [190]

SHOBOLON Giant rat of Romanian mythology. [190]

SIAMANG This term is sometimes applied to the Malaysian mawas, but should in fact be reserved for a kind of gibbon (*Symphalagus syndactylus*) which is 3'/90cm tall and whose existence is not in doubt.

SIANACH Legendary giant and dangerous deer of Scotland, perhaps based on the elk or moose (*Alces alces*) which was once to be found there. [M]

SINAA The hybrid of a human and a jaguar, with eyes set in the back of its head, in the beliefs of the Juruna of Brazil. [M]

SINGAPORE CREATURE Round-shaped creature which remindeed the witness of a beach ball seen walking out of a forested area in 2004. It had arms, a horn on its forehead and feet, which were attached directly to the body without intervening legs. It walked upright. [230]

SINU PARAKEET A Colombian bird which may still survive, but whose existence has not been reported since 1940.

SIYOKOY This is the term used in the Philippine Republic for a kind of merman. It has scaly skin. The female is called *sirena*, a common European term for a mermaid.

SIRIN In Russian legend, this bird has the head and chest of a woman. Its body resembles an owl's. [190]

SKAHNOWA Gigantic breed of turtle in Seneca Indian tradition. [M]

SLEIGHTS CREATURE This was seen in the north of England by two witnesses. The time was about 10.30 at night. The animal, which stared at them, seemed 4' high and 3' wide. It appeared to glide sideways and then out of sight. It was coloured black. [1]

SMALL-HEADED FLYCATCHER A bird (*Sylvania microcephala*) painted by

Audubon. It hasn't been seen since, so its continued existence is in doubt. [#9]

SNAKE-TREE A carnivorous tree allegedly to be found in Mexico. Its existence was reported in the *Illustrated London News* in 1892. [225]

SNOW LION (Tibetan *gangs senge*) These are celestial animals representing joy and bonhomie in Tibetan belief. They have a clearly supernatural character, as their feet are thought never to touch the ground. The body is white, the mane turquoise. [190]

SNOWFLAKE DINOSAUR In 1993 between Snowflake and Heber (Arizona), a 10'-12' reptile was seen by two witnesses running across a road. It reminded one of them of a tyrannosaurus rex. [A6]

SOCIETY ISLAND PARROT It is not certain if this parrot, of which two specimens were caught in the 18th Century, still exists.

SOLAR ENTITY Another name for the rod (see *Dictionary*)/

SOMERSET WHITE CAT A large white cat, the size of an Alsatian/German Shepherd. This is not the only report of such a cat in this English county. [H18]

SOMERSETTE CREATURE A 15-year old was followed through woods in Somersette County (NJ) one night about 1974 by a creature which he could not see. He took shelter until daylight when the creature, which he could not identify, jumped over him and sped off. [154]

SONGY TIGER An out of place animal reported in France in 1910. [155]

SOUTH DAKOTA CENTAUR In one of the parks in South Dakota, there is a rumour amongst the rangers that a couple reported seeing a creature half man and half horse. Details are very vague. [199]

SOUTH ISLAND KOKAKO This subspecies of the kokako was last seen officially in 1967. It is distinguished from the North Island kokako by having orange wattles, while the latter's are blue. The subspecies was officially declared extinct in 2007. However, this declaration may have been premature. In 2006 calls indicative of the bird were heard in the Fiordland region. There have also been reports from Stewart island. In 1996 moss grubbing of the type associated with this bird were found on this island. [200]

SPEED WOLF An extremely swift wolf reported from the area of Buxton (Derbyshire). [146]

SPOOK WOLF In Pennsylvania folklore, a stuffed dead wolf that comes back to life and hunts at night. [225]

SPOONER SHEEPKILLER A large unidentified canid which had apparently been killing sheep in the Spooner Agricultural Research Station in Wisconsin. Although the beast was shot, it was still not possible to identify it. It had surprisingly large teeth and weighed 62 pounds. [G12]

SPOTTSVILLE MONSTER A large humanoid reported from this region of Kentucky. It hung around the farmhouse of a family named Nunnelly. It was blamed for the death of animals, whose carcasses were subsequently avoided by scavengers and even flies. Rose Nunnelly had the first sighting of the creature which was hairy and about 8' tall. One of her sons saw a creature with patchy, red-grey hair. A neighbour claimed to have been spoken to telepathically by the creature when he encountered it. He later claimed to have seen several creatures stepping in and out of a patch of wavy air, like a portal to another dimension. His last sighting was in August, 2004. He claimed that about 1975 he was threatened by the authorities with prison if he went to the media about the matter. [1]

SPREYTON CAT Brindled ABC, the size of an Alsatian/German shepherd, seen in Devon in 2006. [146]

SPRING VALLEY FLYING SERPENT This was reported in New Jersey in 1899 [M12]

SQRAT *Add to Dictionary article* It has now been suggested that, as a hybrid of rat and squirrel is so unlikely, the sqrat may exist, but be a different animal altogether. M. Dawson of the Carnegie Museum of Natural History, Pittsburgh, feels it may be a member of the *Diatomycidae.*

STAG-COW HYBRID Giraldus

Cambrensis (12th Century) said such a hybrid had been produced at Chester. It seemed to fit in well when it joined a herd of cows.

STELLER'S SEA-COW *Add to Dictionary article* A report in the *Chinook Observer* (13th September, 2006), says a sea-captain saw what might have been a specimen off the coast of Washington state.

STERLING BEAST Seen in Illinois in 1938, this animal had a tan coat with yellow spots. It had white shoulders. [A6]

STINSON BEACH SEA SERPENT This animal, estimated at 100' long, was seen from this California locale in 1983. [B9]

STRIX Fierce bird of the night in Roman mythology (Greek *strix*=owl). Its feathers could be used in a magic potion.

STUMPER JUMPER *see* **Wisconsin Pigman.**

STYMPHALIAN BIRDS *Add to Dictionary article* Pausanius (2nd Century AD) claims these creatures were also to be found in Arabia. His source may have been a distorted report of ostriches.

SU SHUANG A bird in Chinese legend, sometimes associated with water.

SUNGAT RENGIT DINOSAUR This was seen about 1976 in Johor by three Malaysian girls. Its height was estimated at 2.5m-3m. While its head resembled that of a tyrannosaurus rex, the eyes were too large to be consistent with this species. The mouth was small and the skin was smooth. [2]

SUPER RAT In Belfast it has been suspected that the brown rat (*Rattus norvegicus*) has developed a super form or mutation that is 22" long and impervious to poison. However, city authorities have denied the truth of this. [*Belfast Telegraph*]

SURMA A beast which guards the Underworld in Finnish mythology.

SUSCON SCREAMER A creature said to be found in the area of Suscon Bridge, Pennsylvania, and to be half pig, half wolf. [216]

SUSSEX COUNTY ANIMAL This

animal, which resembled a kangaroo, was reported from Sussex County (Delaware) in 1979. [M12]

SUSSEX WILDMAN A hominoid, also referred to as the Newhaven BHM, reported from Sussex. A witness, a truck driver with military experience, observed it at Friston Park. It was partially lit up by a red light. He seemed quite sure it wasn't human. [1]

SWAMP APE Name for a BHM used in Georgia (USA).

SWAMP BOOGER Term used for a BHM in the southern USA.

SWAMP MAN Florida name for a BHM.

SWAMP MONSTER Florida name for a BHM.

SWEDISH CREATURE A strange creature with yellow, glowing eyes. It looked like a mix between an ape and a dog. The sighting took place near Stockholm. It was possibly a wolverine (*Gulo gulo*), though these are not usually found in this area. [2]

TACOMA SEA MONSTER A sea monster sighted in the Pacific in 1893. It had an oval body, apparently regular stripes or bands and two protruberances out of which it spouted water that looked like blue flames. There was coarse hair on the upper part of its body. [154]

TACUACHE In Texan legend, a vampire-bat raped a woman in Robstown and this creature was the result. It was supposed to have the face of its unfortunate mother. In everyday Spanish *tacuache* means an opossum.

TAILLESS RACOON A number of racoons (an adult plus some young) have been reported from Chicago recently and they are caudally challenged. This has caused the observer to speculate that they might be a new mutation. [2]

TAILYPO An animal in American folklore. There are sundry variations of the story. A man cuts the tail from a strange creature in the forest, but the animal shows a tendency to come to his cabin by night and demands the return of its "tailypo". Various consequences ensue from this. Whether the tale goes back to some original story of an unknown animal cannot be determined.

TALLAHASSEE CREATURE A humanoid with a large head and shining eyes was seen in mid-road in Tallahassee (Florida) in 1994 by three men, who later returned and saw three creatures. [224]

TAMANGO RIVER MONSTER The carcass of this creature was discovered in the Tamango River on the Chilean-Argentine border in 1907. [210]

TAMPA SEA SERPENT Hypothetical creature which ripped one Dorothy McClatchie to death in the 1920s. Her body was discovered with fierce teeth marks. While more conservative opinion inclined to the belief that the culprit was a shark or barracuda, some ruled these creatures out and voiced the opinion that the injuries had been perpetrated by a sea serpent.

TAOS PUEBLO SNAKE A giant snake allegedly worshipped by the Indians. It was said they sometimes fed it on babies. [200]

TARANDRUS According to Aelian, this

beast resembled an ox with long grey hair. However, it could camouflage itself to look like its surroundings should an enemy appear.

TE TUNA Sea-monster resembling an eel in Tahitian lore. [M]

TEBBI An Ethiopian name for a were-hyena.

TECOLUTA SEA-MONSTER This was found dead on the shore at Tecoluta, Mexico, in 1969. It had a long tusk or horn, was serpentine and weighed 35 tons. Scientists concluded controversially that it was a whale and the corpse was apparently eventually washed out to sea. [120]

TEELGET Monster of Navaho tradition, eventually killed with a lightning arrow. [M]

TEES BAY MONSTER This was seen near Tees Bay, England, about the middle of the 20th Century. [1]

TEINIAGUA A magical lizard in Brazilian folklore which guards the legendary treasure of Salamanca do Jarau.

TENNESSEE CREATURE A human-sized creature covered with hair with a cat's head. It stood upright. It was seen in warren County about 1980. [230]

TENTERFIELD ANIMAL In 2004 this animal, which resembles but is not identical with a rock wallaby, turned up near Tenterfield, Australia. Experts could not identify it. [221]

TERROR OF TUOLUMNE A hominid reported from Pinecrest (California) in 1964.

THELGETH In Navaho legend, these appear to be humanoid monsters lacking heads. This may mean that their heads are held below their shoulders and are consequently undiscernable in poor visibility. They will eat humans. [M]

THOMPSON PTEROSAUR A rock carving near Thompson (Utah) shows what might be a pterosaur, which would mean they survived long enough to be coeval with humans.

THUNDERBIRD *Add to Dictionary
article* Recent sightings of big birds in
North America which might bear out the
thunderbird myth include one in Harrow
(Ontario) in 2003, one in the Ohio Valley in
2004 and one in California in the same
year.

Westmoreland County, Pennsylvania,
has been the locale of a number of
sightings.

Some legends claim that thunderbirds
can become human, some families claiming
thunderbird descent. Certain thunderbird
families were said to live on the north of
Vancouver Island. A Passamaquaddy
legend said a man was blown into the sky
and reached the land of the thunderbirds,
only to discover they were humans with
detachable wings.

Around the beginning of the 16th
Century, there was said to have been a
sighting of the creature at Pennacook (New
Hampshire).

The Winnebago held that thunderbirds
were brightly coloured and that their voices
were like flutes.

A huge bird was seen by a witness in
Weston (Mass.) in 1995. He scoured a
book on avifauna, but could find nothing
like it. [154]

A suggested original for the thunderbird was a huge extinct pterosaur named *Quetzalcoatlus northropi*, some specimens of which may have had a wingspan of about 60'. However, the fossil record does not attest to the existence of this creature after 65 million years ago.

THUNDERSLEY CREATURES
Mysterious doglike creatures seen in Essex in modern times. [146]

TIANMEN CREATURE An animal resembling a turtle with three rows of horns on its shell, eyes like an owl's and a foot-long tail. It was discovered in a reservoir in China in 2006. It has not been identified. [#9]

TIBET DRAGON Two dragons or draconic creatures were photographed over Tibet in 2004. [192]

TIMBER CAT *see* **Woods Cat.**

TINMIUKPUK Gigantic bird in the traditions of the Eskimos of Alaska. [M]

TIPPECANOE RIVER MONSTER
There was a pair of these reported from

Indiana. They were mainly to be found in the vicinity of Devil Swamp and they preyed on livestock. They were of uncouth **appearance and their screams were not of** an enticing nature. After a fight with two hunters, one was killed, while the other fled. [N/S]

TIREE SEA MONSTER A huge long-necked kizardlike creature attacked a boat off this island in 1934. [146]

TOCOPILLA CREATURE Unidentified animal, possibly with wings, seen climbing almost vertical cliffs in Chile in 2000. [224]

TOKOLOSHE I have hitherto avoided listing this creature as too supernatural, but Heuvelmans considers it a cryptid, so perhaps I should include it.

A tokoloshe is hairy and baboon-sized. It is found in southern Africa. Tokoloshes are of a lascivious nature, swift of movement and able to swim or at least float on the water. They can supposedly make themselves invisible. Heuvelmans notes the Africans consider tokoloshes supernatural beings. They are shapeshifters and tend to ravish women.

In South Africa today, many people

sleep on elevated beds, which will fend off the unwanted attentions of the tokoloshe. [C28 H7 K5]

TONGAN GIANT SKINK A supposedly extinct species of skink (*Tachygyia microfloppies*) of which there have been some reported sightings. [N]

TOONGIE Legendary reptilian creature of Papua-New Guinea. [N]

TOOR-ROO-DON This is the name of what was described as a kind of bunyip drawn by an Aborigine named Kurruck in 1847. It looks like an emu. [S11]

TOOTHFISH-EATING KILLER WHALE While it has not been established that this creature exists, it is suspected to lurk in Antarctic waters. [#9]

TOXODON A mammal bearing some resemblance to an hippopotamus, thought to have become extinct in the Pleistocene. However, an artifact from Peru, dating from AD 100-300, has been cited as a possible depiction of this animal, indicating its extinction came much later than is commonly supposed.

TREE MEN In the lore of the Couer d'Alene and Spokane Indians, persons or creatures able to turn themselves into trees and bushes.

TRENTHAM DRIVE CAT An ABC whose coat was tabbyish seen in Asplay (Notts) in 1984. [146]

TRIANGLE CREATURE Creature looking like an upside-down triangle with spindly legs, perhaps a foot in height, seen crossing a road near Lawrence (Kansas). [154]

TSOPO A kind of fierce unicorn of Tibetan belief. [R]

TSUCKINOKO A giant snake of Japanese folklore. Although unrecognised by scientists, many witnesses have reported seeing this creature. In the north it is known as the *bachi-hebi.* [M]

TSUNAMI CREATURE The tsunami which struck south-east Asia in 2004 revealed the remains of a giant unidentified creature. [12]

TUBA (plural *tubae*) A creature that is to be found in Mongolian legend. It has features like a those of a goat and a snail. There have been reports of this animal in modern times. [190]

TUPILAK In the lore of the Eskimos of Greenland, this is a kind of artificial creature. It is made from the skin of an animal which is filled with bones. A magician then brings it to life. [225]

TURKEY CREEK MONSTER Name for a BHM in the region of Sulphur Springs (Texas).

TURNER BEAST This purple-coloured animal met its end when killed by a car in August, 2006, at Turner (Maine). It may have been a dog disfigured in death, but other animals were suggested. It (or something similar) had been previously reported from Androscoggin county. It stared at people with its blue eyes. DNA testing has identified it as a dog, but objections have been raised that it has five toes, the wrong number for such an animal. Some of the reports of the animal compare it to an hyena. A wolverine identity has been suggested, as has that of a fisher. It may be one of a species as beasts with glowing eyes have been reported from nearby woods.

TURSUS A kind of sea monster with human and walrus characteristics which lives in the sea according to Finnish folklore. [R]

TWO-TENTACLED CREATURE This little animal was about 6" in length and propelled itself through the water with a little flap. It had sharp-looking teeth, reminiscent of needles. It was seen in 1998 in a backwater of La Crescent Lock and Dam (Mississippi). [230]

TYCO ANIMAL A strange looking animal seen near the Tyco Electronics establishment in North Carolina. Its head looks like a kangaroo's, its body is somewhat doggish and its tail resembles a rat's. No absolute identification of the creature has as yet been made. One suggestion is that it may be the Mexican hairless breed of dog known as the xoloitzquintle. Witnesses deny that it is simply a fox with mange. There is a kind of red fox with a genetic abnormality known as the Sampson's fox which is hairless and we may here be dealing with such a creature.

Whatever the creature is, it has been suggested there is a population of them in the vicinity of Charleston (SC), but their legs seem too long for them to be foxes and in size it is claimed they can reach the height of a female deer (species unspecified).

TYNEMOUTH SEA SERPENT This was killed off England's North Sea coast in 1849 and put on exhibition in a local shop. [146]

UCHU Monstrous beings in the legends of the Andaman Islanders. When elephants were introduced to the islands, the name was then applied to them. [A.R. Radcliffe-Browne *The Andaman Islanders,* 1922]

UMDHLEBI A cryptobotanic tree which was poisonous and said to be found in Zululand.

UNCLEAN ONE, THE On the Green Path between Robeson and Johnston counties (North Carolina) this bipedal creature has been reported. [200]

UNICORN *Add to Dictionary article* In 1663 what was claimed to be an unicorn skeleton was discovered in a cave in the Harz Mountains, Germany. The cave is now named Einhornhöle after it.

There was an alleged sighting of a unicorn by an 11 year old girl in California in modern times, but I have been unable to procure any details.

A kilin or Chinese unicorn is supposed to have foretold the birth of Confucius. Surprisingly, the kilin was not always depicted with just one horn.

UNKNOWN CREATURE Seen in Calama, Chile, this creature looked like a black Great Dane with wings. It was seen on 10th April, 2001, by a school director. [224]

UNKNOWN FISH An unidentified fish followed a ship off the coast of Wick, Scotland, in 1938. [146]

UNKNOWN JAGUAR In 1996 or 1997 Mark van Roosmalen claimed to have encountered an hitherto unknown species of jaguar in Brazil. [S8/A]

UNKNOWN LORIKEET There is some

evidence that an unknown species of lorikeet exists on New Guinea. The Ketenbangs of that island insist it exists. [A5]

UNKNOWN NIGHTJAR Such birds have been reported from Jamaica.

UNKNOWN RODENT These creatures, which may be feral maras, have been reported from Virginia. [N]

URAYULI Eskimo name for a BHM.

USHI-ONI A name given to various monsters in japanese lore. One of them, a tusked biped, was allegedly killed about 1600. Another type is a sea-monster. [190]

UTAH MYSTERY CAT This was seen by truck driver Ed Bak around 1988. It was larger than a puma and its structure seemed noticeably different. It had a short tail.

VARBERG MOAT MONSTER A small monster said to have been seen in 2006 in the moat of Varberg Fortress, Sweden. [190]

VATA GAM ANIMAL An animal which

resembled, but was unlikely to be (according to officials), a bear, was seen in this part of India in November, 2000. [1]

VAVA'U RAIL A bird of which a drawing was made in 1793, but whose identity is uncertain.

VEKHER Gigantic bird of Russian lore, which was thought to be the origin of the winds.

VEPSKAYA SNAKE A snake rumoured to be found to the north of St Petersburg. Males are said to have some kind of growth on their heads. They can glide from one tree to another and are reputed to be highly poisonous. [#9]

VERI CELEN A polycephalous dragon which could turn into a human in Chuvash belief.

VIBORON Legendary giant rattlesnake in the vicinity of Taos (New Mexico). Its name comes from Spanish *vibora*, 'viper'.

VICKERY CREEK HUMANOID This was seen in 1973 in Papua-New Guinea by Professor G. Opit. He had also heard calls which he took to be those of a large primate on the island. [206]

VIELFRAM German name for the gulon.

VIS A kind of predatory, flying and luminous creature in the folklore of New Britain. It shows some affinity with the ropen. [R]

VLASIAN LAKE MONSTER In 1870 a large monster of draconic appearance was allegedly seen in this Serbian lake. It boasted a cask-sized head and a large tail. It is now perhaps dead, as it seems to be unknown to present day locals. [155]

VOLKHOV RIVER MONSTER
Creature of which a video recording was taken in Great Novgorod, Russia, in 2007. It was a couple of metres or more in length and was coloured grey-white-green. Some have argued that the recording actually shows a trio of creatures. A resemblance to a snake or crocodile was noted. It is thought the monster went into Lake Ilmen. [200]

WAGONER HAIRBALL These creatures, with spiked hair that made them look like hairballs and with black and white fur were seen in Oklahoma in the 1980s. They could run directly up a tree. Their height was that of a medium-sized dig. [230]

WAKADANGI The Omaha and Ponca Indians believe in these creatures. They seem to be primates with long bodies and horns. [201]

WAKINYAN Lakota Indian name for the thunderbird.

WALDOBORO LITTLE MAN
According to a newspaper report printed four months after the original capture, this 18" tall creature was captured in this Maine location in 1855. [N]

WAMPUS CAT *Add to Dictionary article*
An Idaho legend says it has a spiked club on the end of its tail.

WANAQUE BIRD A strange bird seen over Dead Man's Point near Wanaque (NJ). Its wingspan was about 20', but the astounded schoolboy who witnessed it noticed it seemed to have fur rather than feathers. [S20]

WARWICKSHIRE CREATURE Seen in 1995, this creature was reported from Kenilworth Clearing in Warwickshire. It was seen chasing a small deer, than which it was larger. It had spines on its back, small black eyes and a mouthful of menacing teeth resembling needles. In size it called to mind a large greyhound. [154]

WASHINGTON EAGLE A large species of eagle, brown in colour, which naturalist and painter John James Audubon (1785-1851) averred existed. Most modern opinion is that he was mistaken and that he misidentified a subspecies of bald eagle. He claimed to have seen it for the first time in 1814 and in all to have seen it on five occasions. He shot a specimen in Kentucky and examined it with the aid of a Dr Rankin. He said it was 3'7" long and 10'2" across. His description included notable differences from known bald eagles. Washington eagles were said to make their nests in the ground.

Others reported the bird in 1838 and 1842. It was claimed that a specimen was actually kept in captivity by a Dr Hayward.

WASHINGTON HUMANOID The

suburbs of Washington (DC) were allegedly visited by a 12' humanoid in 2000. [2]

WATER DOG In former times this unidentified animal was reported from the Klamath River in the western USA.

WATI-KUTJARA Lizard men in Australian Aboriginal myth.

WATU WA MITI Supposed arboreal primate of Mozambique.

WAUKHEON Sioux name for the thunderbird.

WAYNE LIZARD MAN This creature was reported by a motorist in New Jersey in the 1970s. It was green and scaly. [S20]

WAZOOEY MAN It had red eyes and looked like a haystack. It was reported from Colorado in 1973. [225]

WEJUK An animal of North American Indian legend. It looked like a large black bear and it could throw objects. A sighting by colonial troops occurred on the Vermont/Quebec border in 1759. [N]

WERECAT Belief in the werecat is found in both Europe and America. The kind of cat into which the person changes is a domestic cat.

WERECOW The legendary King Frodo III of prehistoric Denmark, when old and decrepit, was gored by a werecow. [Saxo Grammaticus *Gesta Danorum,* lib. v]. Another werecow was supposed to have helped the Americans against the British in the American War of Independence.

WEREFOX A folktale tells of a witch at Kirklington (Oxfordshire) who was thought to be a werefox. [W7]

WERE-GREYHOUND An informant in the 1920s claimed that he was sure his girlfriend's mother was a were-greyhound and had followed them on their outings. The girl came from Potterne (Wiltshire). [W7]

WEREHORSE A creature of Indiana folklore, said to have acquired the power to fly. [N/S]

WEREPUMPKIN This creature was supposed to have rescued a farmer at

Vincennes (Indiana). [N/S]

WERE-SNOW-LEOPARD In oriental belief, it is held that great lamas can transform themselves into snow-leopards. This was also believed of the Tibetan poet, Milarepa (died about AD 1135).

WERETREE In Northamptonshire folklore witches were sometimes said to turn into trees. [W7] *See also* **Tree Men.**

WESLACO BIRD A large unidentified bird seen near this Texan town on Highway 63 by J. Martinez in 1970. It was coloured brown. [BB]

WEST HECATA ISLAND HUMANOID This creature has been said to be a little larger than a chimpanzee. The island is in Alaska. [X]

WEST ORANGE ANIMAL The witness, without dating the encounter, said he once saw a black-furred creature that looked like a cross between a cat and a wolf at this location in New Jersey. He said the creature jumped over a 6' fence. [S20]

WEST WYCOMBE MONSTER In

2002, part of Buckinghamshire was flooded and, in the floodwaters, some sort of monster was discerned. However, it proved to be a hoax, made from a tractor and car wheels.

WHARTON CREATURE A humanoid animal, hairy and apparently wet, also apparently lacking arms, was seen on a road in Wharton State Forest (NJ) in 1993. [224]

WHAT-IS-IT Originally, this was a title given to a supposed freak put on exhibition by P.T. Barnum (1810-1891). It was intended to look like a subhuman, but was in fact portrayed by persons who were nothing of the kind, the first being Harvey Leech, the second Henry Johnson.

However, it was also applied to a predator in Rumsay (Ca.) which was held to be killing sheep in the late 19th Century. The *Woodland Daily Democrat* felt it was a gorilla, a word that posed orthographical problems for them. It was blamed for stealing and partially eating the heifer of a Mr Clapp, who, on finding the remains, was most chagrined. A large hominid observed by a Mr Gilbert was thought to be the creature.

The term has also been of a tusked

hominid in Mississippi which was pursued by hunters and killed one of their dogs before escaping.

Again, the phrase was used to describe a creature reported in Pennsylvania in 1879. It was said to be almost 4' tall, long armed and toeless, lacking hair. Its colour was yellowish brown and it had horns. Finally, the term was applied to a creature in El Paso (Texas) which turned out to be a piece of artwork by a taxidermist.

WHITE ANIMAL It is about the size of a puma with hair tufts on ears and tail. It has been reported from Kentucky and Pennsylvania. [2]

WHITE CANID Two of these animals were killed by a hunter in Serbia-Montenegro. They could not be identified. They seemed white/grey in colour. They seemed larger than wolves, with heads more canine than a wolf's. [155]

WHITE-FACED BEAR A strange bear, once a human, with a white face and white paws, in the legends of the Aleuts. [221]

WHITE HUMANOID A crayon white humanoid, having holes instead of ears and nose. The eyes were very large, shiny and black. This creature was sighted in Iowa. [223]

WHITE MOUNTAIN CREATURE In 1995 a family intending to camp in the White Mountains (Arizona) were warned by a strange girl to come no further. They turned around and drove back, setting up camp later. Then, into the light of the fire, came a creature with no fur over its skin. It was very thin and looked like just skin and bones. It had sharp teeth. It was the size of a bear. It ran back into the trees. [154]

WHITE ROCK LAKE GOATMAN This lake is in Dallas (Texas) and a goatman, which throws garbage, is said to be found in its vicinity. It is declared to be 7' tall.

WHITE THING A creature noted from the Happy Hollow Road in Alabama. It is white, man-sized or taller and utters piercing screams. It has been known for four generations.
    Do not confuse with the White Thing in *Cryptosup.* [1]

WIGIDOKOWOK A prehuman race in the lore of the Indians of the American northwest. They seem to have had animal characteristics, but the lore concerning them is not clear.

WIKATCHA The Creek Indians believed in this creature, a kind of underwater cat. There seems to have been only one of them. He fathered a child on a human woman. [R]

WILDERNESS CREATURE A creature described as 'huge', seen by a couple in woods adjoining Wilderness, South Africa, in 2003. The female and a neighbour also heard screeching from the wood. The impression given is that the creature they saw was a hominid. They also found in the woods what looked like a dwelling, formed of roots. [154]

WILDMAN Wildman reports from Europe continue to surface. Some loggers were said to have encountered a brace of wildmen in France in 1646. In the French Alps wildmen were called *Sarradons* and in 1958 a local told folklorists his mother had seen them. They used to come into the village of Saint-Maximin to beg. In Germany, human=looking tracks were found in the Odenwald in the 1970s. A humanoid 7.5'-8' tall was seen at Hahn in 1985. It was definitely not a bear. It was brown-red in colour. Two palaeantologists were claimed they were attacked by wildmen in Spain in 1993.

WILDMAN OF NASHAGAK This creature was the subject of much belief in Alaska during the 19th Century. Prospectors avoided the territory where, it was said, he was wont to roam. [A7]

WILKIE Apparently a kind of hominid in Scottish folklore.

WILLIAMSPORT MONSTER A bird with a horse's body, reported from Williamsport (Pa.) in 1909. [N]

WILMORE CREATURE A party fishing at the reservoir at Wilmore (Pa.) saw a non-human figure 7'-8' in height. It was bright white. Its movements made them think its knees were reversed. [244]

WI-LU-GHO-YUK Canadian First Nations legendary creature, which can enter a human's clothing and feast upon the human's body, anaesthetising him so that he doesn't realize what is happening until too late. [203]

WINAXI Winnebago name for a
thunderbird.

WINGED APE An apelike creature with
wings, reported near Tucapol, Chile, in
2000. It had clawed hands and long
protruding fangs, according to the witness.
It was about 4' tall. This animal may be
identical with a creature seen some days
later at Santa Elena de Cocha. [224]

WINGED DEER This was reported in
New Jersey, perhaps about the year 1810.
It is possible it was a sighting of the Jersey
devil. [M12]

WINGED HORSE Pegasus, the winged
horse of Greek mythology, was supposedly
the ancestor of a species of winged horses.
Belief in Pegasus may not have started with
the Greeks, as Pegasus is not a name of
Greek origin. In fact, it may come from
Luwian *pihassis,* 'lightning'. Luwian was
spoken in ancient times in the country now
called Turkey.
    The Romans believed in four winged
horses that drew the chariot of the sun.
They were Pyrois, Eos, Aethon and

Phlegon.

Pliny used the term *pegasus* for a winged horse generally and said they were to be found in Africa.

In Korean myth, there is a swift horse named Chollima, which is sometimes depicted as winged.

The Persians believed in a winged horse called Dadhikra.

At Chimney Rock (North Carolina) in 1811, a number of mountaineers claimed to have seen a battle between cavaliers, mounted on winged horses, in the sky.

WINONA ANIMAL A mysterious beast reported from Winona (Minnesota) in 1919. The animal was said to be the size of a yearling calf. It was grey with stripes. Dogs were afraid of it. [A6]

WINTERFOLD CREATURE This was seen by a driver in Surrey. Its head was oblong and glowing. It was about 140cm tall. It was seen on 16th December, 1967. [146]

WISCONSIN CREATURE A creature seen in the early morning of New Year's day, 2005. It was the size of a doe with a wolflike head. [G12]

WISCONSIN FURRY CREATURES
These could be as large as a kitten or as
small as a mouse. They used to be seen by
the roadside and, with great speed, retreat
into the bushes as the witnesses approached
in their car. They were seen on a number of
occasions some time after 2000. It is
possible that the little ones were the young
of the bigger. [200]

WISCONSIN PIGMAN A creature in
Wisconsin folklore, described as half-man,
half-pig and regarded as affable. *See* in
Dictionary the articles **Pigman** and **South
Georgia Pigman.** This creature has also
been called the *Stumper Jumper.*

WITTENHEIM RADISH It looked like a
radish, black in colour and sliced down the
middle, but it was alive like an animal. It
was seen in France in 1954. A witness was
sure it was a Martian. [224]

WOLF-BEAR CREATURE A creature
that resembles a wolf, but is the size of a
bear, has been reported from a number of
locations in Wisconsin, including Mosinee
and Antigo. [1]

WOLF-FACED MAN A bipedal creature seen in Wisconsin in the 1970s by a couple called Woiak. [G12]

WOLF-HEADED HUMANOID
According to legend, a denizen of Henderson County (Kentucky). [29]

WOODS CAT A long-tailed animal reportedly found in the Shawnee National Forest. Also called timber cats, they are said to be much bigger than a domestic. Some are striped like a tiger, some brown. The tail distinguishes them from bobcats. [A5]

WOODSBURROW WILDMAN A creature similar to, but smaller than, a bigfoot, was reported by campers. Details are unsupplied. It may have been a young bigfoot. [154]

WORCESTERSHIRE CAT A brown ABC with a black face and tail, seen in 2006. [F12]

WUCHWOSEN In Passamaquoddy Indian legend, a huge bird, the flapping of whose wings made the wind blow. [221]

XEXEU South American equivalent of the thunderbird. The Cashmawa Indians credit its existence. [M R]

YACUMAMA A kind of monster, about 50' in length, said to dwell in the Amazon River and nearby.

YAKSA Gigantic humans in Laotian myth.

YAMAGON An animal similar to and perhaps identical with the hibagon of Japan. [B9]

YANN-AN-OED Dangerous water-monster in Breton folklore. [M]

YARDLEY YETI This creature reported from Pennsylvania has been rather unfortunately named as it bears no resemblance to a yeti. It has been described as combining the features of a fox, cougar and jackal and a tail like a rat's. After it was initially reported, the *Bucks County Courier* received a large number of reports of what was said to be the animal.

YARMOUTH MARSH CAT A number of these animals were said to have been seen in this locale in the 1940s. They may have been gigantic feral cats. [F12]

YAROMA In the lore of the Australian Aborigines, huge hairy hominid creatures which could swallow an entire human. They had big feet and short legs and proceeded by jumping, the *membrum virile* of each male striking the ground as it did so. [X]

YARRAM APE Strange primate described as looking like a black ape, seen near Yarram (Victoria) by a cryptozoologist, M. Williams, who managed to take a distant photograph, in 2006. [200]

YEDNIA TIGER Alternative name for the Queensland Tiger (see *Dictionary*).

YELLOW HUMANOID Two of these, proceeding rapidly, were seen at Los Piñas, Chile, in 2001. [224]

YETI *Add to Dictionary article* Some would argue that the yeti sightings are no more than glimpses of the Himalayan brown bear (*Ursus arctos isabllenus*).
   A long and unidentifiable hair was discovered in Bhutan in 2001 and there was

speculation that it was a yeti hair. Analysis revesled the DNA of the hair was unrecognisable.

YILBEGAN A dragon or huge monster with many heads in Siberian belief.

YONGMA Dragon-horses believed to be found on the island of Jeju in Korea.

YOWIE *Add to Dictionary article*
Respected cryptozoologist T. Healy now seems to think there is something paranormal about the yowie. Aborigines say yowies will eat humans. On encountering the yowie, a sort of dread beyond the ordinary strikes some humans.

The name of this animal is unlikely to be connected with English *yowie,* meaning a young ewe. Other equally dubious connections involve the Scottish and Irish pronunciations of *ewe* (*yow* and *yoe* respectively). [#9 X]

YOWIE-WHOWIE In Australian Aboriginal folklore, a nocturnal animal that seems to combine features of lizard and ant. It should not be confused with the humanoid *yowie.* To complicate matters, it is sometimes referred to as a yowie. [190]

YOYOLCHE A term used amongst the Mayas for nocturnal prowling creatures.

YUXA YILAN A kind of snake in Tartar folklore.

ZACAPA CREATURE Seen in 1996 in Guatemala, this humanoid creature was black and hairy with a long tail. The witness thought it had wings. Others reported a bat-like creature in the area. [224]

ZANDVOORT SEA SERPENT This creature was seen off the Dutch coast in 1906. [B9]

ZANESVILLE APE Although this beast was so-called, there is no certainty that it was an ape or that it was an escapee from a circus at Zanesville (Ohio) as was suggested at the time. In fact, it was sighted a hundred miles distant from Zanesville. The only description is that it had eyes like silver dollars and the sounds it made were reminiscent of those of a motor-car. [A7]

ZBURATOR Another name for the zmeu.

(See *Cryptosup*).

ZILANT A draconic creature in the legendry of the vicinity of Kazan, Russia. It is the symbol of that city. Some say there is only a single zilant, some that it is a species.

ZIMITRA A dragon once worshipped by the Wends, who lived in the north of Europe. Their modern descendants are the Sorbs.

ZLATOROG In Slovene legend, a white chamois (or gems, as it is sometimes termed) with golden horns. There is only one of its kind. [D4]

ZMEK A Czech name for a dragon that guards treasure. It was also applied to a money-bringing spirit that looked like a wet bird, often a chicken. [G9]

ZMEOAICA A female zmeu. (See *Cryptosup*).

ZOMOK A kind of huge snake unknown to zoology in Hungarian legend. When it reaches full maturity, a zomok is called a *sarkanykigyo.* [190]

ZOOBIE Name for a BHM used in the vicinity of San Diego (California).

ZUZECA Gigantic serpent in Sioux mythology. [R]

Sources

The source references, except where new, are taken from A Dictionary of Cryptozoology *and* Cryptosup. *This accounts for their apparently chaotic enumeration.*

Periodicals

#1 Animals and Men
#7 Fate Magazine
#9 Fortean Times

Books

A5 Arment *Cryptozoology, Science and Speculation* (2004)
A6 Arment *Cryptozoology and the Investigation of Lesser Known Cryptids* (2006)
A7 Arment *Historical Bigfoot* (2006)
B   Bille *Shadows of Existence* (2006)
BB Rebsamen *Big Bird* (2007)
B9 Bord/Bord *Modern Mysteries of the World* (1985)
C27 Citro *Weird New England* (2005)
F5   Freeman *Explore Dragons* (2006)
F12 Fraser (ed.) *Big Cats in Britain Yearbook 2006* (2006)

G9   Grimm *Teutonic Mythology* (reprinted 1966)

G12 Godfrey *Hunting the American Werewolf* (2006)

K11 Kelleher/Knapp *Hunt for the Skinwalker* (2005)

M   Matthews/Matthews *The Element Encyclopedia of Magical Creatures* (2005)

M12 McCloy/Miller *Phantom of the Pines* (1998)

N   Newman *Encyclopedia of Cryptozoology* (2005)

N/S Newman *Strange Indiana Monsters* (2007)

R   Rose *Giants, Monsters and Dragons* (2001)

R9   Rhys *Celtic Folklore* (1901)

S20 Sceurman/Moran *Weird NJ* (2oo5}

T5   Taylor *Weird Illinois* (2005)

W7   Westwood/Simpson *Lore of the Land* (2005)

X   Healy/Cropper *The Yowie* (2006)

Z   Magasich-Airola/de Beer *America Magica* (2006)

Websites

1   CFZ

2   Cryptozoology.com

12 Farshores

29 Kentucky Cryptids

146 www.paranormaldatabase.com

154 www.paranormal.about.com

155 www.europacz.com

188 www.paranormal.about.com

189 Utah UFO Hunters

190 Wikipedia

191 jasonjrackman.com

192 Strange Encounters

193 about.com

194 Steve's Book of the Not So Grateful
Dead

195 monstermania

196 Cryptid Zoo

197 Mark A. Hall

198. www.worldofthestrange.com

199 www.thesupernaturalworld.com

200 Cryptomundo

201 paranews.net

202 weirdnations.com

203 Folklore Heritage of the Pacific North
West

204 www.clarelibrary.ie

205 www.cryptoworld.com

206 www.strangeperception.com.au

207 Australian Yowie Research

208 Brazilian Folklore Myths and Fantastic
Creatures

209 www.kendo.net

210 Weird Illinois
212 Mystery Magazine
213 Global lake Monster database
214 Monster mania
216 unexplained-mysteries.com
217 Bassou: ape-man and hybrid
218 www.unknown-creatures.com
219 Circle of the Dragon
220 Supernatural World
221 Cabinet of Curiosities
222 Indian Legends
223 Obiwan
224 Humanoid Contact Database (Albert Rosales)
225 www,gcbro.com

Printed in the United Kingdom
by Lightning Source UK Ltd.
120216UK00001B/1